PHOTOGRAPHIC MAKE-UP

By

JACK EMERALD

Associate Institute of British Photographers
Associate Royal Photographic Society

FOUNTAIN PRESS DON

CONTENTS

PHOTOGRAPHIC MAKE-UP

HARRY ROY   *Photograph by the Author*

Section Three

CHARACTER MAKE-UP

Section *Four*

MAKE-UP IN COLOUR PHOTOGRAPHY

Section *Five*

CLINICAL MAKE-UP

The Author gratefully acknowledges the help he has received from many sources, with special thanks to:

MAX FACTOR LIMITED, HOLLYWOOD AND LONDON
UNIVERSAL-INTERNATIONAL FILMS OF AMERICA
GENERAL FILM DISTRIBUTORS
CENTRAL OFFICE OF INFORMATION
CROWN FILM UNIT
CINEGUILD LIMITED
B.B.C. TELEVISION SERVICE
GEORGE BLACKLER, Esq., PINEWOOD STUDIOS
ERNEST TAYLOR, Esq., EALING FILM STUDIOS
ERIC CARTER, Esq., PINEWOOD STUDIOS

Foreword

THE professional photographer has long been aware that the advantages of the art of make-up can apply to portrait photography as much as to cinematography. But many amateur photographers are not so cognisant of how skilled practice in make-up can greatly increase the excellence of their own portrait photography. Or, even if they are conscious of these advantages, they tend to overestimate the difficulties involved in making up their pictures' subjects. The result is that they continue to ignore the possibilities of make-up.

Make-up must begin where nature has left off. Complexions and facial characteristics differ, and every individual presents a different problem. The function of make-up, in photography of any sort, is to fit the face dramatically for the part or pose to be portrayed. In motion picture work, this regularly presents an interesting challenge to the make-up artist, and it can offer an equally inspiring one to the photographer.

The use of make-up to help create dramatic types has been developed to a high degree in the motion picture studios. With a small kit of make-up materials, an average of aesthetic sensibility, and a willing-to-try hand, the photographer can achieve for his subjects equally impressive appearance effects. Once this make-up experiment has been undertaken, the photographer will often find it to be one of the most fascinating aspects of his work.

Success in this field dates back to 1928, when members of Hollywood's Society of Motion Picture Engineers and the Academy of Motion Picture Arts and Sciences called upon my late father, Max Factor, Sr., to conduct tests to ascertain what kind of make-up responded best to the new panchromatic film then being introduced to the motion picture industry. Its merits were obvious. It allowed registry of light and shadow nuances which had been quite beyond the powers of the old ortho-chromatic film. But exhaustive research tests, conducted by my father and myself, and immediately screen-tested in Hollywood studios, indicated that a wholly new kind of make-up would be essential.

This completely new make-up was achieved by my father after months of steady research and creative work. He named it, simply enough, Panchromatic Make-up. A revolutionary feature of it was that its shades fully compensated for some deficiencies in sensitivity to certain colour tones peculiar to Panchromatic film. Another outstanding advantage was that applications of this make-up would register on film under any climatic lighting conditions, either bright or soft.

These qualities enabled the cinematographer to attain more natural and aesthetically desirable results than had ever before been possible. Also, his command of these qualities was a sure one; the make-up tints were constant in themselves, and equally constant in their reaction to light and their shade-tone registry on film.

My father's achievement did not go unrecognised by the Hollywood societies which had called upon his talents; and the Academy of Motion Picture Arts and Sciences quickly honoured him with an Academy Award. Awards from the Academy, to-day affectionately referred to as 'Oscars', are highly valued by Hollywood's personalities, for they truly symbolise achievement in some department of cinema creation.

When Panchromatic film came into general use, it was inevitable that skilled photographers should use the new make-up. There are to-day a number of different kinds.

There is Pan-Cake Make-up, for instance, which was originally manufactured a few years back to meet the demands of the Technicolor film, and which so many photographers who do colour film work now regard as the ideal make-up. And there is Pan-Stik Make-up, perfected to produce a special soft-satin complexion sheen specifically for cinema purposes, but now used by countless photographers.

The correct application of make-up is based primarily on the facial features being made-up. The film actor or actress learns to know the cosmetic needs of his own facial contours ; this is precisely what the photographer, who is his own make-up artist, has to learn for each of his camera subjects. Basic procedures are simple enough. But imagination and boldness of concept must play an important part in the application of make-up. This is especially so to-day, when the photographer has the sure and sensitive registry of colour film to record and perpetuate his achievements.

In his book, *Photographic Make-up*, Mr. Emerald has skilfully concentrated a wealth of information which can serve to further the cause of photographic distinction for both professional and amateur photographer. The volume must appeal, too, to those who esteem superb portrait photography as an art form.

MAX FACTOR, JR.,

Hollywood.

Introduction

IN portraiture to-day the accent is definitely on glamour. Women and most men too, for that matter, want to look a little better than their best in a photograph. Modern photography, in fact, is 'big business' in many senses of the word, for the professional success of the sitter—and often his whole future—may depend very largely on just how well a photographic artist has been able to 'gild the lily'.

In the good old days, the soft-focus lens, together with some diligent afterwork on the negative, did most of the 'gilding'. But with the advent of motion pictures and the birth of the publicity 'still', soft-focus effects became practically extinct. They were rapidly replaced by photographs which were critically sharp throughout and which showed every detail of face, figure and costume.

These publicity photographs, although vastly superior to anything previously seen in this line, nevertheless increased the problems of negative retouching to a considerable extent. In the motion picture studio, where speed of delivery of the finished article is of vital importance, the retouching problem was quickly solved; and, for many years, this industry has been expert in the art of making film-stars look glamorous in a photograph and on the screen.

The secret, of course, is clever photographic make-up, or that branch of the science of cosmetics in which the human features can be emphasised, improved or completely altered at will. The film industry has been working this kind of miracle on human material for nearly forty years; but the portrait photographer, to-day such a close ally of his 'movie' colleague, has until comparatively recently neglected the tremendous possibilities of this art.

The time-honoured method, still in vogue with hundreds of first-class photographers, is to take the picture and then go to work on the negative with knife and pencil, removing a wrinkle here, or a piece of the jawline there. Negative retouching is not only tedious but costly; and the result more often than not is a complete elimination of facial characteristics which were part and parcel of the personality of the sitter.

Most people know a heavily retouched photograph the moment they see it: a fact which, among other things, becomes a source of embarrassment to the sitter. To-day, however, this problem can be largely solved by the use of photographic make-up, a medium that is steadily becoming part of the everyday working equipment of an ever-increasing number of portraitists throughout the world. Thus the lily is gilded first; the photographer becomes an expert make-up artist and, as a result, his work is halved to the satisfaction of all concerned.

I have specialised for many years in the art of cosmetics in portraiture, and in this book I propose to give the reader a practical guide to this particular technique which, I am convinced, he will find an improvement on other methods. Retouching the features of a sitter beforehand by the use of suitable make-up is a far more satisfactory method of altering facial structure than retouching the surface of the negative afterwards. Apart from the more artistic effect that it is possible to create, it has the advantage that the individual sitter can see for himself, or herself, how the initial adjustments are being made; to what extent they enhance the appearance; and whether or not they get near to satisfying the inherent human desire to look one's impossible best.

Photographers who use make-up for portraiture are

unanimous in the opinion that this preliminary treatment helps to put the sitter at ease. My own experience has always proved this to be so; but the cosmetics must be applied with discretion and by a photographer who thoroughly knows his job.

Throughout the history of mankind the human desire to alter facial and physical characteristics by the use of dyes and pigments has persisted with each succeeding generation from the days of the woad-painted Britons to the present day. Although there is no precise data regarding make-up through the ages, it can be safely assumed that the pictorial value of the medium has remained, for all practical purposes, unchanged. What has changed—and is still changing with the march of science—is the process of manufacture and the technique of the application of cosmetics.

In general no hard and fast rules exist in make-up. It is true that a careful study of the technique of application will carry the beginner safely through the initial stage of the art, but from then on it is only constant study and practice that will bring its own reward.

With this in view the co-operation of acknowledged experts in the art of make-up was sought in an effort to illustrate pictorially the various types of make-up dealt with in this book. This help was immediately and enthusiastically given, and I would like to acknowledge gratefully the valuable advice and information given me by the Max Factor Organisation both in this country and abroad. Without such help, a book of this description would inevitably be incomplete, for the obvious reason that the views and opinions of any one person could hardly be comprehensive in such a controversial subject as make-up.

With the exception of fish-skin, the cosmetics and all accessories mentioned in the book are easily obtainable from high-class chemists, make-up and fancy dress stores or the manufacturers direct.

In including in the text such items as fish-skin and the collodions, I had in mind completeness of subject rather than practical necessity. At the moment, fish-skin is extremely difficult to obtain; but then so are a great many other things which, let us hope, will be more plentiful soon.

Basic Make-up Technique

MAKE-UP FOR WOMEN

IN turning to the study of make-up, the portraitist is probably urged by the desire to eliminate, as far as possible, the necessity for negative retouching, though later perhaps, as he acquires more skill and his interest deepens, he will begin to experiment in character studies and other aspects of the art.

Most photographers devote a considerable proportion of their waking hours to the problems of negative retouching. I believe that a mere fraction of that time diverted to study of this chapter alone will eventually produce better results.

TECHNIQUE OF APPLICATION

In the application of photographic make-up, the first step is to make sure that the face of the model has been thoroughly cleansed of all street make-up. This serves the double purpose of revealing the structural composition of the features and, at the same time, removing stale cosmetics.

The removal of street make-up is best done by working cold-cream well into the face with the tips of the fingers, then wiping off with face tissues or cotton wool. When all trace of street make-up has been removed, apply an astringent such as skin freshener to the entire surface of the face. This will remove the greasy effect of the cold cream.

We are now ready to apply the foundation colour.

The secret of a perfect make-up is the foundation. Photographic make-up consists, in some cases, of as many as six skilfully blended colours, thereby making the pigment Panchromatic, or light-sensitive to all colours of the spectrum and it is intended to reproduce as a satin smooth skin in the finished print.

Clever highlighting, flawless shading and perfectly shaped lips will not help much unless the foundation is right. Both with grease-paint and Pan-Cake Make-up, the aim must be smoothness and transparency.

With grease-paint foundation you should first squeeze a small amount of colour from the tube into the palm of the left hand; less than half-an-inch of colour is sufficient to cover completely the average-sized face. Then with the second finger of your right hand, take a little of the colour, and apply to the forehead, temples, cheeks, nose and chin with light taps, or stippling movements.

Work these dabs of colour well into the skin, taking great care to spread the colour smoothly, evenly and sparingly, until the entire surface of the face, from the hairline to well under the chin, is covered with a thin, even film of monotone colour. Continue this smoothing process, working from the centre of the forehead outwards to either side; then work from between the eyebrows up and into the hairline: down the centre and either side of the nose, and from the inner corner of each eye outward and over the cheeks in a half-circular movement. Smooth downwards over the cheeks, and continue downwards over and under the jawline. From the lower lip, smooth over and under the chin.

18

This smoothing process will remove all surplus colour and leave the skin with an appearance of silky texture. Pay particular attention to the inner corners of the eyes and the sides of the nostrils. Above all, avoid patchiness.

The cake foundation colour is applied with a moist sponge if desired over an Invisible Make-up Foundation after the face has been cleansed in the manner described for grease-paint. A touch of this invisible make-up on the forehead, a touch on the cheeks and a final touch on the chin is sufficient. In no circumstances should more than this small amount be used. Blend these spots of invisible make-up over the entire face until no trace of the make-up is visible.

Now moisten the sponge. Wring some of the water from it, but not all. Rub the sponge briskly in a circular movement round the surface of the foundation colour, until a creamy consistency is obtained; then apply quickly, thinly and evenly to the whole surface of the face. As with grease-paint foundation, work for smoothness and transparency. Blend the colour well up into the hairline with the finger tips, then over the chin and sides of the jaw to well down the neck.

PAN-STIK MAKE-UP

Pan-Stik Make-up is a non-greasy, cream base make-up in unique stick form. It can be applied in just a few seconds, resists perspiration, can be retouched and repaired without removing the entire make-up, and never presents a heavy or 'masky' appearance. Pan-Stik Make-up supplies a satin-smooth complexion tone when powdered, or a soft, warmly glowing sheen if left unpowdered.

19

Pan-Stik should be swivelled from its container until it is just slightly exposed. Apply several light strokes to forehead, nose, cheeks, and chin, using it sparingly. With the finger-tips, blend the original touches of Pan-Stik upward and outward until the application evenly and very thinly covers the entire face, and down below the chin line. Pat on face powder and brush away excess with a powder brush. To retouch or refreshen, wipe away the surface layer of the make-up with a cleansing tissue. Apply Pan-Stik lightly, blend it with the finger tips into the rest of the make-up, and then powder. Dirt smudges and streaks can be removed easily with a damp cloth or tissue.

HIGHLIGHTING

In smoothing and blending the foundation colour into the natural hollows and crevices of the features, we have carried out a kind of levelling up process. We have, in effect, created a new photographic skin of smooth even texture, the very evenness of which—unrelieved by any areas of lighter, or darker, colour—appears slightly to flatten the features. It is therefore necessary to remodel the contours of the face by means of highlighting and shading.

You may ask, 'Why go to all the trouble of creating a nice new photographic skin with make-up if this, in turn, destroys the natural contours and modelling of the features and makes further make-up necessary to restore these characteristics?'

The answer is simple. In removing the natural modelling and characteristics from the face, we remove all facial blemishes such as spots, moles, lines and wrinkles at the same time. Then by means of highlighting and shading, we can restore the characteristics and re-model the features, leaving the unwanted spots and blemishes completely out of the picture.

All corrective treatment must take place at this stage. Further details of this will be found in a later chapter. In a basic, or fundamental, make-up no corrective treatment is necessary.

Highlights are usually placed as follows: (1) Down the centre of the nose. (2) On the chin. (3) Along the edges of the cheekbones just below the outer corners of the eyes. (4) Above the eyebrows. Although I myself prefer to use plain white cosmetic for highlighting, it is better to begin by using a shade three or four shades lighter than the foundation colour.

Apply grease-paint highlights with a flat-top sable brush and carefully blend with the tip of the finger. Blend the edges of the highlight into a fadeaway effect with the foundation colour. Apply the cake highlight colour with the edge of a moist sponge and blend as for grease-paint.

Correctly applied and blended, it is almost impossible to distinguish between the highlighted areas and the foundation colour. Don't let this worry you though; the camera will record the highlights quite satisfactorily.

For shading the face see "Corrective Make-up" section.

EYE-SHADOW

Eye-shadow is applied to the eyelids with a flat-top sable brush. Some make-up workers favour using the tip of the little finger; but in view of the extreme sensitivity of the eyelids a sable brush application is far more comfortable from the sitter's point of view, and is the safest method for a beginner in make-up.

A small amount of the colour should be placed on the eyelid close to and almost touching the eyelashes. It should then be blended upwards into a fadeaway effect below the eyebrows. A very steady hand is required for

21

this job. For a basic make-up, use eye-shadow very sparingly indeed.

With the eye-shadows in place, take a lining pencil and draw a thin line along the upper eyelid touching the eyelashes. Begin the line about one-eighth of an inch from the inner corner of the eye and continue along the full length of the eyelid to a point just beyond the outer corner slanting slightly upwards. Blend this line—using a flat-top sable brush for the purpose—into a fadeaway effect with the eye-shadow, leaving the darkest portion at the point where the line touches the eyelashes.

Now draw a similar line under the eye, close to and touching the lower eyelashes. Begin this line at the inner corner of the eye at a point corresponding with the upper line and continue along the lower eyelid to just beyond the outer corner slanting upwards as before. Never slant upper—or lower—eye-line downwards.

Blend the lower line carefully, making quite sure no flesh is visible between the line and the lower eyelashes.

POWDERING

After the foundation colour, highlighting and eye make-up, comes powdering. Apply powder liberally with a large soft velour puff after first requesting the model to close her eyes. See that powder reaches the crevices at the sides of the nostrils and at the inner corners of the eyes. Leave the powder on the face for a few moments and then brush off all surplus powder with a powder brush.

After thoroughly brushing off all surplus powder, it is an excellent plan to apply a skin freshener. Blending powders are more matt than otherwise when applied to the foundation pigments. The skin freshener will remove the matt effect by restoring a slight sheen to the skin. A few drops of skin freshener on a cotton wool pad patted lightly over the surface of the features is all that is required.

The eyebrows are shaped with an eyebrow pencil, every effort being made to follow the original curve of the brow. The eyebrow should be re-fashioned by a series of fine lines and never created in the form of a curved line with one swing of the pencil. The pencil must be finely pointed and used to tint the actual hairs of the brow rather than the flesh in between. If necessary, the lines may be extended above, or beyond, the natural growth of the brow. It should be borne in mind that the final effect must look natural and not exaggerated.

Begin re-shaping at the nose end of the brow after first making sure that all surplus powder has been removed from between the hairs, and continue working along the full length of the brow to a point beyond the outer corner of the eye. Always keep to the original curve of the brow, and, above all, do not extend the brow too far beyond the outer corner of the eye.

LIP-COLOUR AND ITS USE

The lips—together with the eyes—form the expression of the human face. Great care and discretion must therefore be exercised where the re-styling of lips is concerned. Apply the colour with a lip brush. Fashion the upper lip first, following the natural curve of the lip. Work carefully, beginning immediately beneath the bow of the lip.

With the lip brush charged with colour, steady the hand against the side of the face. Apply some of the colour from the brush on to the lip just under the bow. Then, with the colour remaining on the brush, begin to fashion the bow. Work from the base of the lip upwards, approaching the apex of the bow with great care but avoiding the 'Cupid's bow' effect.

If too thin, the upper lip may be extended above the natural lip-line, although care must be exercised to see

23

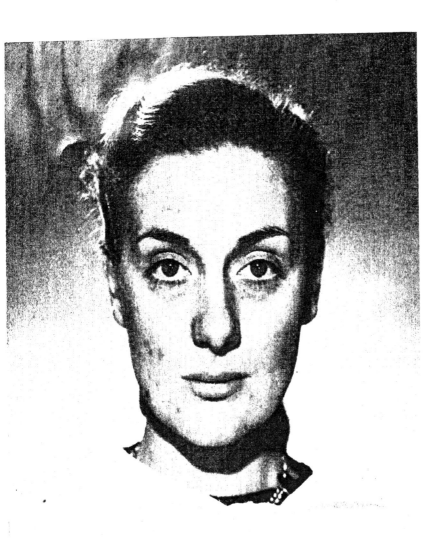

BASIC MAKE-UP TECHNIQUE

1 Before make-up has been applied. Note dark areas under the eyes and angry spots on surface of the skin.

2 Applying Pan-Cake foundation colour with a moist sponge.

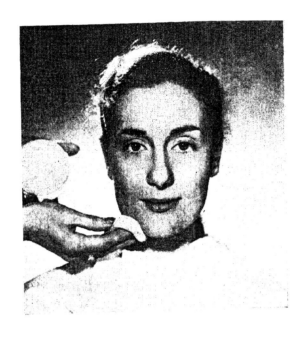

3 Eye-shadow is applied to the upper eye-lids with the tip of the little finger.

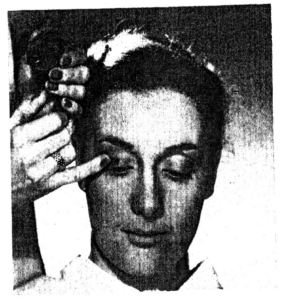

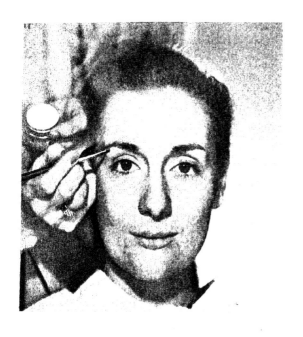

4 Apply highlights with a flat-top sable brush.

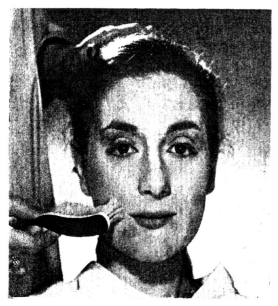

5 Apply powder liberally with a soft puff and brush off all surplus with a powder brush.

6 A line is drawn upon the upper and lower eyelids close to, and touching, the eye-lashes with a brown lining pencil.

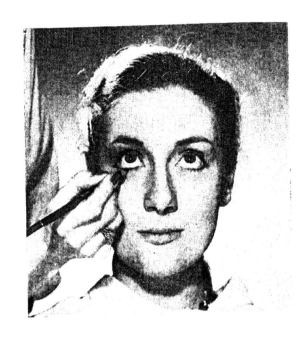

7 The eyebrows are shaped with an eyebrow pencil, every effort being made to follow the original curve of the brow.

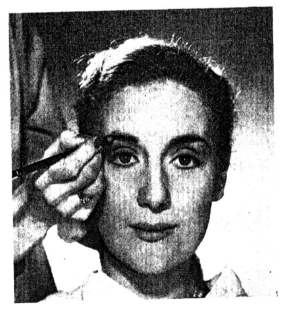

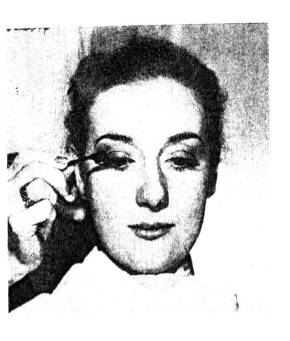

8 Apply mascara with a brush. First brush the lashes downwards to remove any surplus powder and then upwards over the upper eyelids.

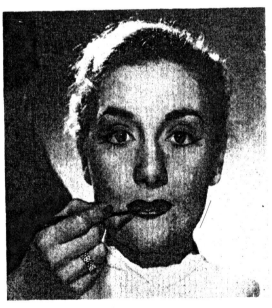

9 Lip colour is applied with a lip brush. The lower lip should be full and well shaped; the upper lip, if too thin, may be extended above the natural lip-line.

10 After the make-up has been completed. Compare with same model before make-up was applied, page 24.

that the extended portion still follows the natural curve of the lip. The lower lip should be full and well shaped. Do not powder the lips after the colour has been applied.

MASCARA AND ITS USE

The final stage in a basic photographic make-up is the application of eyelash make-up to the eyelashes. Mascara serves the double purpose of accentuating the eyelashes and adding lustre or brilliance to the eyes. The majority of models prefer to do this part of make-up for themselves but, when you have to do it for them, proceed as follows:

Apply mascara sparingly with a brush. Moisten the brush and charge with colour. First brush the eyelashes downwards to remove any surplus powder, then upwards over the upper eyelids. The lashes should be separated and evenly blackened with colour. Blobs of mascara are not only unsightly but complicate matters still further by depositing spots of black colour on the upper eyelids with every blink of the eyes.

False eyelashes, with rare exceptions, should not be worn in portraiture.

Here then is the fundamental—or basic—photographic make-up for a woman. Practise applying it as often as you can to enable you to develop that flexibility of the fingers so necessary for the comfort of the model and the manipulation of the different colours.

With continued practice you will soon find that you begin to know the 'feel' of the human face, the position and formation of the bone structure which, in turn, will teach you all you need to know about highlights and shadows. You will begin to learn something of the beauty of human eyes and how to portray their beauty to the fullest advantage; and you will see the sensitivity and mobility of the lips and the part they play in the character of the features as a whole.

As you smooth and blend the pigments over the surface of the features, you will begin to experience a feeling of pride—a pride in your ability to frame the beauty, strength, and character of the human face attractively. For that is the fundamental principle of all basic and corrective make-up technique—to frame attractively that which is already there and not hide the true character and personality of the sitter beneath a mask of cosmetics. It is my firm opinion that a *basic* make-up is the most that can be actually *taught* of the art of make-up. For the rest, there are no hard and fast rules. Two artists may place a shadow in two different places on the face and yet achieve a similar result.

One can be taught to play the piano but it doesn't necessarily follow that the practice of scales and exercises alone is a sufficient guarantee of future virtuosity. In basic make-up then will be found the scales and arpeggios of eventual make-up virtuosity. All that is required is the practice and interest necessary to develop the inspirational touch.

MAKE-UP FOR MEN

With the exception of character studies and certain branches of colour photography, the use of photographic make-up for men sitters—if necessary at all—should be confined to bare essentials.

To begin with, most men look upon make-up of any kind as a purely feminine habit, and the thought of having it applied to their faces, even as a photographic aid, is repugnant. Pointed remarks about its glamorizing effects only make matters worse and bring forth an outburst of manly wrath little short of catastrophic to the success of the sitting.

In the main, a cake foundation sponged quickly and lightly over the surface of the features will adequately take care of excessively oily or shiny skin or even that photographic bugbear, the blue chin. Even this minute amount of make-up should be applied only after the position has been clearly explained to the sitter and his consent obtained.

Assuming he does consent, sponge the cake over the surface of the features as quickly as possible and make sure that the colour does not clog the eyebrows or eyelashes nor cover the lips. If this does occur, remove it with clean moist cotton wool.

Use the normal male tone of cake colour and apply sparingly.

After the application, brush the surface of the features vigorously with the powder brush. This will remove excess colour from the little lines and crevices which are an important characteristic of the masculine face. Do not apply any powder unless requested by the sitter.

Oddly enough, men's faces could often be improved from the photographer's standpoint with a carefully applied make-up. On the motion picture set no self-respecting artist, man or woman, would dream of taking part in a 'scene' without first receiving an impeccable make-up.

But in the portrait studio, particularly in this country, photographic make-up is comparatively new; and male sitters, even professionals from the worlds of theatre and screen, can find no connection between being photographed and having a photographic make-up applied to the surface of their features; hence the somewhat suspicious attitude of the male sitter towards any suggestion of make-up as a photographic aid.

I have already stressed the importance of the psychological effect of make-up. But this can work two ways. With most women it can be extremely good; with most men it can have an entirely opposite effect. This being so, tread warily with men and make-up.

JIMMY EDWARDS

Photograph by the Author

SECTION TWO

Corrective Technique

IN the previous chapter I described the technique of fundamental, or basic, photographic make-up for women. The principal function of this type of make-up is to emphasise existing characteristics; and, for this reason it is used only when the model's features conform to accepted standards of beauty. Just exactly what constitutes the accepted standard of womanly beauty is largely a matter of opinion. Some hold, for example, that the ideal face should be oval in shape and possess regular features. For the purpose of clarification and convenience in deciding whether basic or corrective technique is required, it is necessary to identify the type or classification of the face before the application of cosmetics.

FACE SHAPES

The shape of any face can usually be identified with one of the following groups; oval, round, oblong, square, triangle and inverted triangle. There are several other shapes, but as these are mostly owned by all-in-wrestlers and boxers, we are hardly concerned with them here!

It has already been emphasised that no hard and fast rules exist in make-up. The art of cosmetics, which must include theatrical character work as well as beautification, is really the art of creating, by a skilful blend of coloured pigments, an impression of beauty or ugliness, youth or age, reality or fantasy, according to the requirements

35

of a given situation. Thus, in correcting or improving the existing facial structure of a sitter, the make-up artist is really creating an impression corresponding to his own or somebody else's conception of the pattern to which the facial structure in question should conform. And a successful result can be secured only by the skilful blending of highlights and shadows.

The re-shaping of facial contour is simple if it is borne in mind that highlights broaden the features and shadows narrow them. This is the governing principle of all corrective make-up treatment.

There are innumerable ways in which the features of a model may require corrective treatment. For example, a face could be triangular in shape, the nose too broad, the eyes too close together, and the lips thin and irregular, while in another triangular face the nose could be too thin and the eyes be too far apart. It is by no means impossible to think up a dozen different variations of corrective treatment which might be necessary for either of these types of face.

To attempt to do so and, at the same time, describe the corrective make-up treatment required in each instance would be confusing. I therefore propose to take a series of hypothetical faces in their various shapes and then in their component parts, and to deal with each part separately under its own heading.

RE-MODELLING TRIANGULAR FACE CONTOURS

Of all the facial contours requiring corrective treatment perhaps the most common is the 'triangle-shaped' face, the prominent feature of which is the extreme width of the jawline creating an impression of narrowness in the upper section of the face. The main problem confronting the make-up artist here is one of broadening the forehead and at the same time reducing the width of the jaws.

All corrective make-up treatment begins with the application of the foundation colour. Working on the principle that highlights broaden and shadows narrow, it is necessary to use on the forehead a foundation one shade lighter in colour than on the rest of the face.

Apply the normal colour first, using the light taps or stippling movements described for a basic make-up. Stipple the colour on to the cheeks, nose, chin and jawline, but for the time being leave the forehead untouched. Blend and smooth the colour from a point in line with the eyebrows down the face, over the chin and jawline, to well down the neck.

Now take a colour one shade lighter than the normal colour and apply to the forehead. Blend this lighter colour well up into the hairline, across the forehead, down the temples into a fadeaway effect with the normal colour, and just above the nose. Then take a colour at least four shades darker than the normal foundation colour and apply at a point just below the ear towards the side of the face.

Blend this darker colour inwards in a half-circle corresponding with, and just below, the line of the cheek. Do not, in any circumstances, allow the colour to creep over the cheekline on to the cheek itself. Blend the colour inwards until a point midway between the side of the face and the nose is reached, then blend down the side of the face, and over the jawline. Blend under the jawline to include part of the neck. If the chin is too prominent, extend the darker colour to include the chin, blending down over and under the chin to the neck.

With the blending of the darker colour, or shading, completed, stand back about three feet from the model and study the effect of the corrective make-up treatment. At this distance it should seem to have noticeably reduced the width of the jaws and correspondingly

37

increased the width of the forehead. Look for any sign of a line at the point where the darker colour meets the normal foundation colour; and if any such line is visible, pat and smooth until it disappears. Be sure to work from the line to the side of the face and never towards the centre of the face.

Now study the effect once more. Is the shading too dark? If so, then too much of the darker colour has been applied. Remove some with plain cotton wool and re-blend the remainder. If the shading is hardly noticeable at all, then an insufficient amount of darker colour was added and more is required.

Check and re-check your work until, from a distance of three feet, you get a distinct impression of balance between the width of the forehead and the jawline. When you are satisfied that this is so, carry on with the rest of the make-up.

RE-MODELLING THE INVERTED TRIANGLE FACE

The 'inverted triangle' face is that in which a broad forehead narrows down to a pointed chin. Corrective make-up here is intended to lessen the width of the forehead with shading and, by the use of highlighting to add roundness to the lower part of the face.

First apply the normal foundation colour to the lower section of the features from a point level with the eyebrows. Smooth and blend in the correct manner. Then take a colour one shade darker than the normal foundation colour and apply to the forehead. Smooth and blend this darker colour up into the hairline, across the forehead, down the sides of the temples and just above the nose. It is better to blend from the nose upwards, at this point, rather than from the forehead downwards, because the darker colouring could quite easily alter the shape of the nose.

Having blended the forehead foundation colour, it is now necessary to deepen the shadow at the sides of the forehead and thus reduce the width still further. This deeper shadow is achieved by the use of a colour at least four shades darker than the normal foundation colour. Apply the shadow to the sides of the forehead to a width of between one and two inches, according to the width of the forehead. Carefully blend the inner edges of this shadow, working towards the side and never towards the centre of the forehead. This completes the reduction of width in the upper part of the face.

It is now necessary by the use of highlighting to add roundness to the lower part of the features. For this use a colour four shades lighter than the normal foundation colour and apply first to the natural hollows in the cheeks and carefully blend the edges of the highlight with the foundation colour. Highlight from a point just below the ears down the side of the face, and over and under the jawline and chin to include part of the neck. Blend this highlight inwards over the chin, and slightly inwards over the jawline towards the corners of the mouth. Carefully blend the edges of the highlight into a fade-away effect with the foundation colour. Accent the line of the jaw and rounded part of the chin with a thin line of white colour and blend over and under the chin and jawline, but not inwards towards the face.

With foundation colour, shading and highlighting completed, apply eye-shadow and then powder the features with a normal shade of powder for the lower part of the face, and a powder one shade darker in colour for the forehead. Do not apply powder until you are quite satisfied that all shading and highlights have been correctly blended and that, from a distance of three feet, the make-up appears to have effected a decided improvement all round. Complete remainder of make-up.

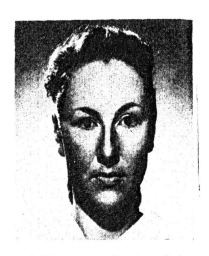

1 Before make-up. Note the round wide jawline and spots on the skin. Compare with completed make-up opposite.

2 Foundation colour is applied and blended over the entire surface of the skin.

3 Corrective shading roughed in one each side of the nose, the hollows of the face and jawline.

4 Side view of corrective shading.

CORRECTIVE MAKE-UP

Corrective make-up completed

The round or moon-shaped face, no rare phenomenon in portraiture, responds to a remarkable degree to corrective make-up treatment. With very little difficulty, the round face can be re-modelled into an attractive oval or heart-shaped face.

Foundation colour of a normal shade is applied to the features in the usual way and blended from well up into the hairline downwards over the entire surface of the features to well down the neck.

Shade with a colour four shades deeper than the foundation colour. Apply the shadow to each side of the face near the lobe of the ear and continue to blend inwards following a half circle line just below the line of the cheekbone to a point midway between the nose and the side of the face. Now blend the shadow backwards and downwards in a slightly curving pattern over and under the jawline. Blend the shadow under the chin, but do not allow any trace of the darker colour to creep on to the chin itself. From the lobe of the ear, blend the shadow upwards, keeping well to the side of the face, to a point level with the eyebrows. Pat and smooth the edges of the shadow into a fadeaway effect with the foundation colour.

RE-MODELLING THE SQUARE FACE

Fortunately, the square face is seldom encountered in the portrait studio, which is just as well, because this type of face calls for corrective make-up treatment of an exacting kind. It demands all the most competent artist's skill and taste. In brief, one's aim must be, by means of suitable shading, to change the square into an oval.

Apply the normal foundation colour, smoothing and blending in the prescribed way. It is particularly important to take sufficient time over the blending in order to give one an opportunity to note mentally the exact positions for subsequent shading.

In shading a square face, begin by placing a shadow at each side of the forehead. Use a colour several shades deeper than the foundation colour and place the shadow diagonally and curving away from the middle of the forehead. The upper part of the shadow, of course, is the wide portion of the diagonal and should extend inwards from the side of the head to a width of between an inch to an inch and a half. The lower part of the shadow meets the hair at the sides of the temple.

Pat-blend the edges of this shadow. Smoothing movements will only destroy the effect of the curving diagonal, thereby undoing part of the corrective treatment. Blend well into the hairline at both the top and sides of the forehead. When the blending of this forehead shadow has been completed, highlight the full length of the actual diagonal curve of the shadow—that is, from the point where the diagonal curve was pat-blended with the foundation colour.

The highlight should be little more than a quarter of an inch in width throughout its full length and should be two or three shades lighter in colour than the foundation colour. Carefully blend the two edges of the highlight on the left side with the shadow area and on the right side with the foundation colour.

Highlighting a shadow in this way tends to deepen the shadow still further, provided, of course, that the brightness range of the highlight in question is sufficient to attract the eye away from the shadow area. Only constant practice can teach the beginner the correct degree of brightness necessary for the highlighting of shadow areas.

The lower portion of the features should be given corrective treatment in harmony with that for the upper part of the face. The squareness of the jawline must be shaded down and highlights added to effect roundness and modelling. Place the shadow at the side of the face close to the ear, using a colour four shades deeper in colour than the normal foundation. Blend the shadows inwards in a curving pattern just below the natural line of the cheekbone to a point midway between the nose and the side of the face. Then blend the shadow backwards and downwards over the jawline and under the chin, but in no circumstances must this chinline shadow be allowed to creep on to the chin itself. Pat-blend the facial edges of the shadow into a fadeaway effect with the normal foundation colour and the lower edges with the neck colour.

Highlight the edges of the cheekbone just below the outer corners of the eyes and carefully blend. Highlight the chin itself and the point at both sides of the chin at which the shadow has been blended with the foundation colour. Pat-blend the edges of these highlights. Use a colour four shades lighter than the foundation colour and apply highlights with a flat-top sable brush.

RE-MODELLING THE CHIN

The Double Chin. Apply the normal foundation first and carefully blend. Subdue the double chin by placing a shadow on the appropriate part of the chin and blending right round under the jawline. Use a shading colour for this purpose.

Receding Chin. Apply normal foundation colour. Place a thin line of shadow in the natural hollow just below the lower lip and pat-blend. Highlight the receding part of the chin. Powder the chin with a lighter shade of powder than for the rest of the face.

Prominent Chin. Subdue prominence of the chin by using a foundation deeper in colour than for the rest of the face. Unless the chin is very prominent, one or two shades deeper should be sufficient. Powder with a corresponding shade of powder.

Pointed Chin. Use a foundation colour one shade lighter in colour than for the rest of the face. Place a highlight round the edge of the chin and blend with the foundation colour. Powder with a corresponding shade of powder, i.e. one shade lighter than for the rest of the face.

Cleft Chin. Apply normal foundation colour to the entire surface of the features and carefully blend. Place a strong highlight in the cleft of the chin with a flat-top sable brush and blend. Use white pigment for highlighting cleft chins. Also highlight the lower edge of the chin. Powder with a normal blending powder.

The re-styling of eyes is by far the most difficult step in corrective make-up. Slight errors of judgment in highlighting and shading are to a certain extent permissible, and will probably go unnoticed in the finished print. But faulty workmanship with eye make-up would be glaringly obvious in the same print, and if scrapped negatives and constant retakes are to be avoided, it is essential to form a clear mental picture beforehand of the precise type of corrective treatment required and how such treatment will affect the eyes in their relationship with the features as a whole.

It is generally acknowledged that, ideally, the human eyes should be exactly the width of one eye apart; and although some experts contest this, the theory is useful enough as a guide.

It is not within the power of the make-up artist to beautify the eyes. Nature bestows a degree of perfection beyond the range of human improvement. But the make-up artist can frame the eyes in the most attractive way possible. Eye make-up is applied to precisely the same places for corrective purposes as is necessary for a basic make-up—that is to the upper and lower eyelids, the inner and outer corners of the eyes, and the eyelashes.

45

Before attempting any re-styling of the composition and structure of eyelids, etc., be certain that they need it. When in doubt, apply a basic eye make-up and let this suffice. Study the photographs supplied by the Max Factor Make-up Studio to illustrate the eye make-up worn by models A, B and C on page 47. Of the eye make-up designed for these three models, Hollywood make-up stylist Max Factor Jr. writes as follows:

1. The eyes of model A are naturally large and their size is apparently increased by an exceptionally broad and wide eye socket structure. This calls for carrying eye-shadow applications all the way up to the brow itself, rather than confining the shadow to the lid alone. This eye-shadow application is kept away from the socket structure, as this borders in towards the nose. As this area is deep set it is naturally shadowed by its own deepness. The eyelashes are finer than average, so they need make-up applied more heavily than usual. An eye-brow pencil line is drawn at the base of the lower lashes (considerably more heavily than is advisable for most women), and then blended with the fingertips into a faint but rather broad shadow effect. This shadowing serves to make the eyes seem even larger than they are, but is primarily created to provide a tone balance for the shadow so broadly applied on and above the upper lids.

2. The eyebrows and eyelashes of model B are of a sturdy thick hair growth which require that make-up be applied very thinly. She needs just enough to establish a degree of darkness which will offer colour-tone contrast with the skin for photographic purposes. With a small eye-socket structure, eye-shadow is applied to the upper lid only. None is applied on the socket area above the lid. To make the socket area seem larger, with this in turn making the eyes seem larger too, a heavy apparency of brow growth at the inner tips is 'lifted'

46

EYE MAKE-UP

Photographs supplied by The Max Factor Make-up Studio, Hollywood.

MODEL A

MODEL B

MODEL C

47

by plucking on the under edges. The height of the brow arch is then increased by pencilling in the middle section on the upper edge.

3. Model C has eyelashes which are actually as fine as those of model A, but they are so unusually long and this makes them so obvious to the onlooker, that an extra heaviness of make-up application is not needed. The eye-socket structure is of average dimensions, so no shadow is used above the upper lids, and no major alteration of eyebrow shape or arch is required.

These are excellent examples of the make-up methods of a creative artist. The underlying moral is: adapt your make-up technique to suit the individual character and personality of the model and do not—as is sometimes attempted—adapt the character and personality of the model to suit the make-up.

EYES TOO CLOSE TOGETHER

Where the eyes of a model appear to be too close together or to require special attention in other ways, I have found the following method satisfactory.

Apply eye-shadow to the upper eyelids with a flat-top sable brush and blend upwards and outwards, towards the outer corners of the eyes. Continue to brush-blend until the eye-shadow is considerably fainter at the inner corner or nose area of the eye, and somewhat heavier at the outer corner. Then, with the lining pencil, draw a thin line on the upper eyelid touching the eye-lashes. Begin the line about a third of the way in from the inner corner of the eye and continue along the remaining length of the eyelid to a point just beyond the outer corner of the eye. Brush-blend this line so that, like the eye-shadow, it is fainter at the inner corner of the eye and heavier at the outer corner. Begin to blend at the point where the line commences a third of the way in from the inner corner of the eye. First brush some of the colour over on to the clean area of the eyelid and then along the full length of the lid to the outer corner of the eye.

The idea of starting the line so far in from the inner corner is to make sure that the colour in this area will eventually become the faintest of faint shadows.

EYES TOO FAR APART

The corrective treatment in this case is a reversal of the foregoing. Apply eye-shadow to the upper eyelids and blend more heavily towards the inner corners of the eyes and considerably more faintly towards the outer corners. Line both the upper and lower eyelids, beginning the line in each case at the inner corner of the eye and continuing along the full length of the eyelid but gradually fading the lines away as they approach the outer corners of the eyes. Brush-blend the lower eyeline until it becomes a faint shadow touching the lower eyelashes.

DEEP-SET OR SUNKEN EYES

Eye-shadow must *not* be used for deep-set eyes otherwise the sunken effect will be increased instead of decreased. At the most, the eyes may be outlined with an eye-lining pencil, but only upon the upper eyelid until such time as the mascara has been applied to the eyelashes. If, after the application of mascara, the eyes appear to be too small, the lower eyeline should be drawn and carefully blended into a faint shadow effect. Highlight the area of the eyelid immediately above the socket area of the upper eyelids and brush-blend with the foundation colour.

PUFFY EYELIDS

Apply eye-shadow in the normal way and brush-blend into a fadeaway effect upwards towards the eyebrows.

Then, with the brush, apply a heavier film of colour, if you wish, a deeper shade of colour, to the area of the eyelids immediately above the eyes. Blend this film of deeper colour upwards, gradually fading it away into the lighter tone eye-shadow. Ask the model to close her eyes at frequent intervals to enable you to check the result as you continue to blend. Line both upper and lower eyelids with a lining pencil. Blend the lines into a subtle shadow touching the eyelashes.

RE-SHAPING THE NOSE

Re-shaping the nose is not a difficult problem. It consists, in the main, of highlighting down the centre of the nose to broaden or lengthen it, and shading at the sides and tip to lessen the width or length. Side shading is also useful in creating a convincing third dimensional effect.

Occasionally, the nose of the model will be well proportioned and will require no treatment other than the application of a normal foundation make-up. For instance, model D on page 53, has a perfectly proportioned nose, in the classic-patrician pattern, and Max Factor Jr. reports that this lovely feature is made-up exactly like the rest of her face. No highlighting or shadow illusions of any sort are required.

The nose of model E is shadowed at the sides, above the nostrils, in an up-and-down straight-line pattern of shadow application, which apparently lengthens her nose.

The nose of model F is treated by applying shadow out on the cheek areas bordering the nose, with the in-toward-the-nose edge of this shadow application terminating sharply at the point where the definition line is desired. Further definition is achieved by highlighting the side of the nose in the area adjoining the sharp-edge stop of the small shadow application on the inner curves of the cheeks.

The illustrations on page 53 show the effectiveness of nose highlighting and shading.

NOSE TOO BROAD

Apply shadow to the sides of the nose with a flat-top sable brush. Use a colour three or four shades deeper than the normal foundation colour and blend from the nostrils upwards towards the bridge of the nose. Begin shading the nostrils first and then extend the shadow to whatever point appears necessary—which will depend upon whether the nose is too broad throughout its full length or only partly so.

Highlight the outer edge of the shadow and blend with the foundation colour on the inner curve of the cheek. Blend the inner edge of the shadow with the foundation colour on the nose. Powder the nose with a powder one shade deeper in colour than for the rest of the face.

NOSE TOO LONG

Apply normal foundation colour first, then apply a shadow to the base of the nose and blend upwards and over the tip to the point where the line of definition is desired.

NOSE TOO THIN

Use a foundation one shade lighter in colour than for the rest of the face. Highlight the sides of the nose in an up-and-down pattern of highlight application from the nostrils to the bridge of the nose. Powder the nose with a powder one shade lighter in colour than for the rest of the face.

NOSE TOO SHORT

After blending normal foundation colour, apply a long thin strip of highlight straight down the centre of the nose from just above the bridge to a point just below the tip of the nose. Powder with a normal blending powder.

Apply normal foundation colour and blend. Highlight straight down the centre of the nose as far as the turned-up part and carefully blend. Shade the turned-up part with a colour one shade deeper than the foundation colour. Powder the nose with a normal blending powder.

HOOKED NOSE

Apply normal foundation colour and blend. Apply a colour one shade deeper than the foundation colour to the apex of the hook and blend with a flat-top sable brush. Highlight above and below the hook in an up-and-down straight-line pattern. Keep both shadow and highlight to the centre of the nose throughout its full length. Do not allow the blending of either highlight or shadow to creep over the sides of the nose.

MAKING UP THE LIPS

The curve of the mouth and shape of the lips are probably, with the exception of the eyes and voice, the most obvious physical manifestation of mood, character and temperament. Joy and tragedy, elation and sorrow, aloofness and sensuality, are all revealed in mouth and lips.

So it will be seen that in attempting to re-style the lips, the make-up artist is batting on a very sticky wicket. There are no rules. The majority of make-up artists like to work on the assumption that the lips are non-existent and then later to decide which lip-shape would be most suitable and to fashion mouth and lips accordingly. Admittedly this method calls for a modicum of practical experience, but it is the only successful one.

There are, of course, faces which present no such problems. Of model G on page 55, Max Factor, Jr. observes that every feature of this model's face is of such perfect structure and proportion that she could advantageously present any form of lipstick pattern she might

NOSE MAKE-UP

Photographs supplied by The Max Factor Make-up Studio, Hollywood (see page 50)

MODEL D

MODEL E

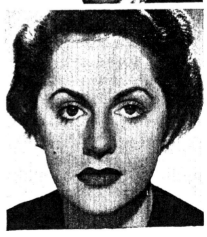

MODEL F

desire. The pattern she prefers, however, is the one shown on the opposite page, because she believes it is the most dramatic. It has a slight 'pout effect' to its arch, which proves particularly appealing. This hint of a pout is one of the most difficult effects to achieve. On most women it makes them look unattractively sullen.

The broad 'hunters' bow' lipstick pattern of model H is not a pointless stylism, but a deliberate artifice to narrow her lower jaw area by lessening the expanse of white complexion between mouth and jawline. The lip-stick shades depend upon the shade of hair of the model.

The lipstick pattern of model I is styled to make her upper lip seem longer. The upper lipstick pattern is kept thin, with a deep V-dip at the centre.

GENERAL POINTS FOR LIP RE-STYLING

With a full or broad jawline re-style the lips to the full width of the mouth. If the natural lip-line is on the small side, extend the colour above and below the natural line of the lips. Be careful not to allow the shape to droop at the outer corners of the lips. Drooping corners create an impression of sorrow or tragedy. If anything, a very slight upward tilt should be given.

The thin upper lip, the most common of all lip problems, should always be re-fashioned and the lip-colour extended above the natural lip-line. If this is not done and colour is applied to the actual line of the lip the upper lip will almost completely disappear in a smiling pose or in any position where the head is in a downward tilt. Profile positions also quickly disclose a thin lip unless the feature is corrected.

REMOVAL OF WRINKLES

First apply a N.1 foundation colour grease-paint to the entire surface of the features and blend well into the

STYLE IN
LIP MAKE-UP

Photographs supplied by the Max Factor Make-up Studio, Hollywood.

MODEL G

MODEL H

MODEL I

skin. Then, with the first finger and thumb of your left hand, squeeze the lines or wrinkles of the fore-head together until they become miniature valleys. Now, with a small pad of clean cotton wool in your right hand, begin to wipe the colour from the top and sides of the valleys. Begin at the right-hand side of the forehead (your right-hand side not the model's) and work right across the forehead with a squeeze-wipe movement, an inch at a time. Next take the wrinkles at the corners of the eyes. Squeeze and wipe as before. Renew the cotton wool frequently and work over the entire surface of the features in this way, squeezing and wiping until most of the light colour has been removed from every part of the face except the seat of the lines and wrinkles. Pay particular attention to the smile lines which stretch from the nostrils to the corners of the mouth. When all the light foundation colour has been removed, take the normal foundation colour and apply a little to the back of your left hand; about half-an-inch squeezed from the tube should be sufficient. With the ball of the second finger of your right hand work this colour around until it has a thin creamy appearance. Then, with the first finger and thumb of your left hand, squeeze the wrinkles of the forehead together exactly as before, and with the second finger of your right hand, begin smoothing the normal foundation colour across the forehead in a kind of squeeze-smooth movement. Smooth quickly and lightly, working from right to left as before. Treat the whole of the face in this way, squeezing and smoothing until the whole of the features from the hairline to well under the chin has been covered with the normal foundation colour and until the seat of the valleys created by the squeezing together of the lines still retains the lighter colouring.

This is by far the best and easiest method of removing smaller lines and wrinkles. After all a wrinkle is only noticeable at all because shadow is formed in minute valleys of flesh. Remove the shadow and the wrinkle

56

at once disappears—or seems to do so. By squeezing the lines together and thereby retaining the N.1 foundation colour at the seat of the line the shadow is eliminated and will not record as a wrinkle in the finished print.

The larger areas of lines, such as the smile lines from the nostrils to the corners of the mouth, may be further highlighted with white colour applied with a flat-top sable brush when the normal foundation colour has been applied and blended.

Summary

For the rest, there is very little that an ordinary foundation make-up won't take care of. Spots, blemishes, blackheads, and small pimples completely disappear with the blending of the foundation colour.

Corrective make-up was designed by experts to assist in the successful making of motion pictures. The photographic success of motion pictures is a sufficient guide to the effectiveness or failure of a method of photographic control possible with an average amount of intelligence and a kit of photographic make-up. Study the 'stills' outside your local cinema. Look for the subtle highlighting and shading used in the make-up; then go inside and look at the same things magnified a hundred diameters or so.

In this chapter I have enumerated the various facial flaws most likely to set retouching problems to the average portrait photographer. In suggesting the virtues of corrective make-up I write as one who has found, after many years of trial and error, that photographic make-up can put into a portrait what negative retouching can never achieve. Make-up can accentuate character just where such accentuation will be most telling, that is, in the mind of the sitter. Can retouching ever do this? I think not.

The various methods I have described are not to be taken as the only ones; but they are the methods I use

KIMM KENDALL. An example of effective lip make-up.

Photograph by the Autho

STEPHANIE VOSS. The lip-styling must at all times be suited to the character portrayed.

Photograph by the Author

myself and have always found satisfactory. Every artist evolves his own methods; and this book is intended merely as a guide for the reader in his own early experiments. After all, this is precisely what is happening with the manufacturers and make-up experts throughout the world. Every day new suggestions and ideas are tested and either put into use if successful or discarded if impracticable. This is how the whole art of make-up has been evolved; by experiments conducted by people with an artistic sense and the pioneer spirit.

Character Make-up

IN all make-up technique—whether straight, corrective or character—the basic bone structure of the face is a constant factor. It may be emphasised, improved, or even exaggerated; but it must never be ignored or violated. Exactness in placing highlights and shadows brings added emphasis to youthful beauty, but it is just as necessary when making-up a face to simulate old age. Improvise as often, as freely and as fantastically as you like, but be careful that your work never deviates from the face's structural composition.

CRÊPE HAIR

Character work introduces the beginner to several new make-up materials. The first of these, and one which is usually experimented with more often than any other, is crêpe hair, which is used to create false beards, moustaches, sideboards and bushy eyebrows. In fact, it can be used wherever hair is desired and is non-existent— whether on face, hands or body.

It is sold in plaited hanks which should be unwound at one end and thoroughly combed out some hours before use. Putting it between the folds of a damp towel overnight will materially assist in straightening out the kinks. Several different shades should be bought; beards and moustaches are seldom identical in colour with the hair of

STEPHANIE VOSS in juvenile character make-up.   *Photograph by the Author*

the head, and it is therefore as well to be prepared before-hand.

The hair, when ready for use, is applied to the flesh and fixed with spirit gum, a fixative specially manu-factured for use with make-up. Spirit gum is a good adhesive.

APPLYING HAIR TO THE FACE

False hair is applied to the face as follows. Spirit gum is brushed lightly on to the appropriate area of the flesh and allowed a few moments in which to become partially dry and 'tacky.' A small quantity of the crêpe hair is cut from the main hank, trimmed, and then pressed into position on the gum-painted area of flesh. The hair is held firmly against the flesh for a moment, during which it becomes firmly 'fixed' by the spirit gum.

CREATING A BEARD WITH CRÊPE HAIR

The make-up artist creates and fashions false beards with the same skill and exactitude that he applies to his other make-up techniques.

A careful study of beards and moustaches reveals that the hairs grow in a distinctive pattern, and that their colour differs from that of the hair of the head. Moreover, whiskers have a tendency to huddle together in certain areas and be sparse in others. To produce a realistic print therefore, the false beard must be built up in a pattern similar to that to which it would conform if left to grow by itself—the only difference, of course, being that the make-up artist does the job a great deal quicker than nature.

Usually the colour of a beard is a little lighter than that of the hair of the head. Select and prepare the crêpe hair accordingly; a shade lighter in colour than the hair of the model's head. Then apply the foundation grease-paint to the surface of the features and blend in all areas of the skin other than that to which the false beard and moustache is to be applied. With the foundation colour blended, leave highlighting and shading and the rest of the make-up until after the beard has been applied.

Next, with a small brush, paint spirit gum on to a small area of the flesh directly underneath the chin. Then take up a small bundle of crêpe hair from the flattened-out end of the skein (about forty or fifty hairs is sufficient) and cut off a six-inch length. Trim the top end (the end where the length was cut from the main hank) and with either a towel or a spatula press the hairs gently but firmly against the previously painted, and by now quite 'tacky,' spirit gum area. Cut another six-inch length of forty or so hairs and fix into position immediately to one side and touching the first lot. A further six-inch length should then be cut and fixed into position on the other side of the centre strip. Now trim the free end of the sections by cutting off about an inch of the hair just to even the ends up, as it were; don't try trimming to the actual desired length at this stage. Next, apply more spirit gum to the area of flesh immediately above the attached hairs, which should be approximately on the base of the chin itself. Cut off a slightly shorter (about five inches) length of hairs from the hank and attach as before, after allowing the spirit gum to become 'tacky.' Cut two further five-inch lengths of hair from the main hank and attach one on each side of the centre hairs on the chin-line.

After these two lower layers of the beard have been attached begin building up the beard, first on one side of the face and then on the other; but interweave a few light hairs on all top layers of beard, gradually increasing the amount in the moustache and chin area. The illustrations clearly show the extent to which these lighter hairs should be interwoven with the darker ones.

Always build up the beard with overlapping layers of hair, applying the lowest layer first and the highest, or

64

top, layer last. The moustache should be applied last of all.

Roughly trim the lower ends of the beard as you go along and reserve the final, and correct length, trim for when the whole beard has been attached.

The moustache is created by applying two lengths of crêpe hair, side by side, on the upper lip; then combing them apart and downwards into the hair of the beard. Later, the hair of the moustache should be trimmed on the underside around the edges of the lips.

When the whole of the false beard and moustache has been attached and trimmed to correct size a curling iron should be heated and the hairs waved to complete the illusion if necessary. The lower layers of hair should be waved first, and the upper or top layers last. But don't over-do the waving.

After the final trimming and waving, you can lightly brush both beard and moustache all over with spirit gum, but only if a very set effect is desired. This will 'set' the hairs more firmly together and thereby minimise the danger of displacement by a casual movement on the part of the model.

Highlights and shadows may now be added to complete the make-up. These are more easily achieved with flat-top sable brushes because, in character studies, highlighting and shading are used more subtly than in a basic or corrective make-up.

In the illustrations on pages 66 and 67 I have deliberately selected a model with a rather 'full' face, well covered with flesh. Examination of Fig. 6 will show how highlights and shadows have been built up to create an impression of loss of flesh consistent with the implied age of the character created. Mr. Jack Faint, who kindly posed for the illustrations, is in the early thirties, whereas in Fig. 6 the implied age is somewhere between fifty and sixty. No attempt was made to heighten the illusion of age by partially greying Mr. Faint's thick and somewhat luxuriant head of hair. Had I done so, the illusion

CHARACTER MAKE-UP

1 Mr. Jack Faint before character make-up and crêpe hair is applied.

2 Building up the false beard with crêpe hair. Begin under the chin first and build up with lengths of the hair.

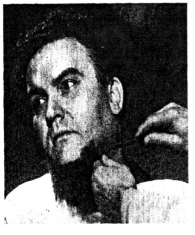

3 Attaching the crêpe hair to the side of the face and 'fixing' with spirit gum.

4 The completed beard and moustache in place before final trim and waving.

5 The completed hirsute creation with moderate character make-up applied.

6 Highlighting and shading strengthened to create an impression of loss of flesh and a scar added to dramatise the effect.

of age would have been considerably heightened; but at the expense of minimising the power of highlighting and shading to create the effect alone, I decided to omit this final 'touch'.

In the motion picture industry, where realism is the main consideration, no effort is spared in the attempt to reproduce the minutest characteristics of old age. For example, Stuart Freeborn, talented young make-up man at Pinewood Studios, had a most exacting job in Cineguild's screen version of Charles Dickens's 'Oliver Twist'. He had to transform Alec Guinness's features into the evil visage of Fagin, whom Dickens described as 'very old and shrivelled . . . a villainous looking and repulsive face obscured by a quantity of matted red hair. He was dressed in a greasy flannel gown, with his throat bare . . .' Experiments for this formidable transformation were based on Cruikshank's famous illustrations, and were started as early as February, 1947.

Even after much practice Stuart Freeborn still took over three hours to complete this complicated make-up. So that when Alec Guinness was needed on the set at 8.30 for the start of a normal day's filming, both he and Stuart Freeborn had to leave their homes at four o'clock in the morning. In fact, Alec confesses that he usually had to catch up on his sleep while he was being made-up.

The most difficult item was the nose. Of outsize dimensions, it was in itself a result of many experiments. Eventually a cast was taken of Alec Guinness's own face and on that mould Fagin's nose was built up. Made from a spongy plastic substance, it was first moulded on to this specially built plaster cast and then baked and painted. Its texture was very similar to that of human skin, and air channels were packed with cotton wool to absorb any perspiration.

Freeborn always had several noses standing by, each of which would last for three or four days' filming. Spirit gum fixed the nose into position but its edges were so thin that very little 'patching up' was needed. Eyebags of this same special plastic came next, and were applied in the same way. The whole face was first painted with a plastic liquid which formed wrinkles as it dried, and then, with the help of grease-paint, was made-up according to a carefully prepared chart, which showed exactly what colours had to go on any one part. Then Alec was given false eyebrows, an unkempt beard, a moustache, and a ragged wig, all of which had to be stuck on separately and had later to be combed to keep up the illusion of unbroken continuity, day after day.

But even then he was not through. Some of his teeth had to be blackened to give the impression of a repulsive toothless mouth. Then one or two fingernails were also blackened, and the make-up was complete. Once made-up, he had to stay put for the rest of the day's filming. During the lunch and tea breaks he experienced the greatest difficulty when drinking, as his nose tended to get submerged in cup or glass. In fact, he could never get used to that enormous nose !

A MAKE-UP EXPERT

Obviously much skill and a painstaking regard for detail was necessary for this job. But Stuart Freeborn began humbly enough. In 1936 he was working as a clerk in the office of a rubber company. Ever since his schooldays he had wanted to do film make-up. For weeks he tried each studio in turn but never managed to get past the man at the gate. So he vowed that he would learn all he could for the next year, and then try again.

He managed to pick up an old field camera for five shillings and spent his modest savings on wigs, grease-paints and a new lamp. All day long he worked as a

ALEC GUINNESS. The remarkable transformation of this famous actor into Charles Dickens's character, Fagin (in Cineguilds' Screen version of Oliver Twist) is shown on the following pages.

1 Fitting the false nose in place.

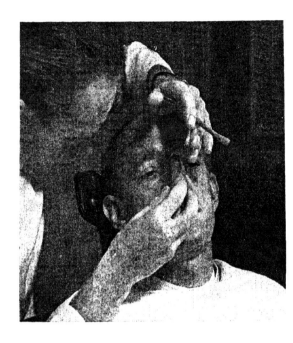

2 The nose in position, Stuart Freeborn applies plastic bags under Alec Guinness's eyes.

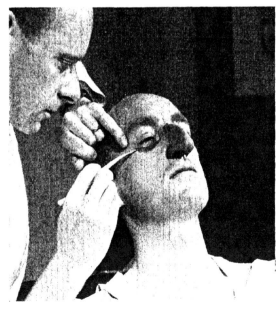

FIRST STAGES OF 'FAGIN' MAKE-UP

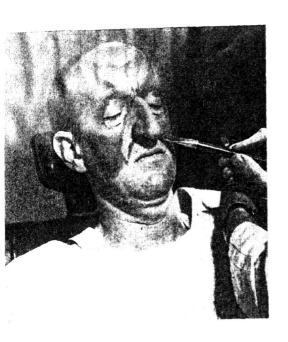

3 Highlights and shadows are 'built-up' to change entire facial structure.

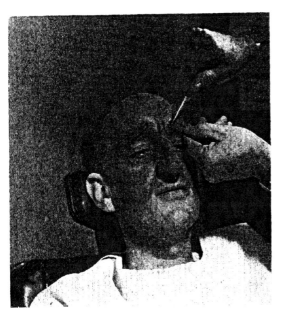

4 New eyebrows are created with crêpe hair.

ADDITION OF HIGHLIGHTS, SHADOWS AND EYEBROWS

5 The matted beard is 'built-up' piece by piece on the face.

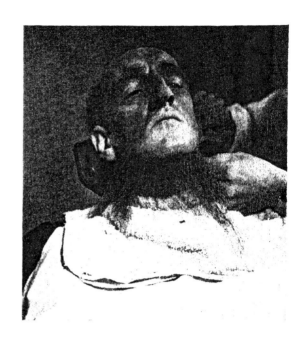

6 The moustache is carefully positioned and affixed.

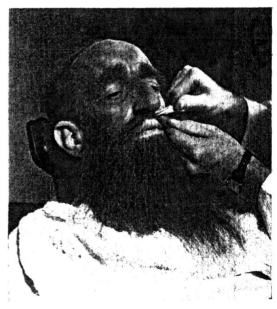

THE BEARD AND MOUSTACHE ARE ADDED

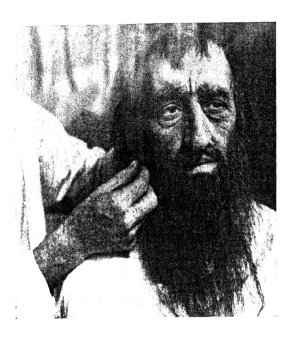

7 The wig is placed in position.

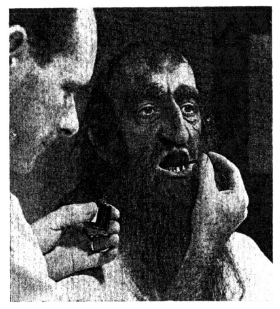

8 Teeth are 'blacked-out' with tooth enamel.

HAIR AND TEETH MAKE-UP

9 The same dye used for his teeth blacks some of Alec Guinness's nails. Such details cannot be overlooked by the camera.

10 Back in his dressing room after his three-and-a-half-hour make-up, Alec Guinness, dressed now in Fagin's filthy rags, shows the result of his transformation to his dresser.

THE FINISHING TOUCHES FOR 'FAGIN'

clerk: every evening he practised making himself up as anything from a Frankenstein to a barmaid, and then fixed up his camera and lighting to photograph himself. His night's work did not finish there. He spent the early hours of the morning developing his pictures.

At the end of the year he had quite a miscellany of character stills. According to plan, he sent every British studio a copy of each, but without result. Sometime later, however, he gave a make-up demonstration at his local camera club; a journalist happened to be present, and Stuart and his stills duly became the subject of an article. Determined to succeed, Stuart thereupon sent each studio a copy of the paper in which the article appeared, but again he heard nothing.

Some weeks later he read in the paper that a new studio had opened at Denham. He determined to have one last attempt and this time he received an answer. Three days later he started work at the new Denham Studios, and has since been responsible for the make-up on such famous productions as 'Henry V', 'Caesar and Cleopatra,' 'Captain Boycott' and 'Oliver Twist.'

RECONSTRUCTING THE FACIAL STRUCTURE

There are several methods of creating old-age effects in make-up character studies. The latest and most favoured is to reconstruct the entire facial structure of the model in latex, a rubberised material similar in texture to human skin. The inner side of the mask is an exact replica of the mould of the model's features, and when applied to the face is a skin-tight fit. The outer side, of course, is constructed to represent the age desired. The mask is attached to the features, make-up applied to the rubberised surface, and a specially-constructed wig completes the illusion. The operation takes, from start to finish, anything between three to four hours.

Another method is to reconstruct part of the features such as the nose, forehead, chin and neck, using a spongy plastic substance also with a texture similar to that of human skin. This spongy plastic substance is attached to the features and held in place with spirit gum; make-up is then applied and the inevitable wig completes the illusion.

CREATING OLD-AGE EFFECTS

Creating old-age effects calls for some knowledge of the anatomy of the human face. It is not sufficient to draw a few heavy dark lines purporting to be wrinkles, stick a tuft of white crêpe hair over each eyebrow and then rely upon a wig of some kind to complete the illusion. That might suffice for a third-rate melodrama but in a photograph would produce a ludicrous result. Lines, wrinkles, loss of flesh shading, together with highlighting of skin seemingly stretched tight across the frontal bone, must all be effected with the utmost regard for detail.

OLD-AGE MAKE-UP

Apply a colour several shades deeper than the normal foundation colour to the surface of the features and blend well into the skin in the following areas; across the forehead wherever there appears to be the slightest sign of any natural wrinkle or line, no matter how faint; at the corners of the eyes in the crows-feet area, that is, the outer corners just above the cheekbone; under the eyes; between the eyes; and on the area where the smile-lines run from the base of the nose to the corners of the mouth. Blend the colour well into these areas, but do not blend up into the hairline when working across the forehead.

Next, take a clean pad of cotton wool and, squeezing

the flesh of the forehead together with the thumb and first finger of your left hand, begin wiping the remaining colour from the surface of the skin. The squeezing together of the flesh will trap sufficient of the dark colour to accentuate natural lines and wrinkles in the skin of the model in a pattern strictly in accordance with the pattern to which those lines and wrinkles would ultimately follow, in that particular face, later on in life.

Work over the whole of the features in this way, squeezing and wiping until all surplus colour has been removed, and all that remains is a series of dark and greatly accentuated lines, crows-feet and wrinkles. Renew the cotton wool as often as necessary to 'clean' thoroughly all other areas of the skin.

Next apply the normal foundation colour. Squeeze the lined areas together as before and apply the colour with a light, smoothing movement. Begin on the forehead, squeezing and smooth-blending from right to left and, this time, blending the colour well up into the hairline. Continue squeezing and blending until all the foundation colour has been applied to the features from the hairline to the neck.

If it is desired to apply false hair of any kind such as a beard, moustache or eyebrows, on sections of the features 'built-up' and exaggerated with cotton wool and collodion, such work must be done at this stage. If not, and the effect desired is a little beyond middle-age, then the illusion can be completed with the necessary highlighting and shading. To get an effect of advanced old age, a collodion and cotton wool make-up is some-times necessary.

The following highlighting and shading will create a satisfactory effect of skin stretched tightly over the facial bones and hollows. Highlight the bone structure of the cheekbones, the frontal bone and all the way round the jawbone. The highlights should be fairly prominent and the edges carefully blended with the foundation colour. The most suitable shade for this type of highlighting is plain white.

Apply the highlights with a flat-top sable brush, and begin on the forehead. Brush-blend a strong highlight from the inner corners of each eyebrow just above the brow and slanting upwards towards the sides of the forehead. Place another strip of highlight around the top edge of the brow itself and touching the brow. Run a highlight straight down the centre of the nose, making it somewhat stronger in the bridge area and a fraction fainter towards the tip of the nose. Highlight the outer sides of the smile-lines which run from the base of the nose towards the corners of the mouth. This highlight should be fairly wide and run from a point at the corners of the mouth upwards towards the inner corners of the eyes. Additional highlights may be added after shading.

Use deep brown or grey colour for old-age shading. Place a strong shadow in the hollows of the temples, the hollows of the cheeks and in the smile-lines. Fainter and far more subtle shadows should be placed under the eyes, above the eyebrows at the inner corners slanting very slightly upwards, and on the sides of the nose.

Brush-blend these shadows very carefully indeed and highlight the edges of the stronger ones, such as the cheek hollows and the smile-lines. When the blending has been completed, view the result and accentuate the following places: above the eyebrows, the inner corners below the eyes, slanting downwards towards the cheeks, and the hollows of the temples. Complete make-up with a normal shade of blending powder.

The youth-to-old-age method of make-up most likely to appeal to the beginner is probably the far more straight-forward highlighting and shading job, with or without the addition of a collodion and cotton wool build-up. Collodion, for use in make-up, is sold in two forms, flexible and non-flexible, both of which have distinct and separate uses which should not be confused.

Flexible collodion is a colourless liquid consisting of ether, alcohol, castor oil and resin. It is highly inflammable and therefore should never be used near a naked light. Its main solvent is ether, and one must therefore be careful not to risk anaesthetising the model; windows and doors should be kept open while it is being applied.

In character make-up it is often necessary to create a double-chin, a bulging forehead, bags under the eyes* and so forth. This is where flexible collodion is useful. It should be first painted on to the area of the skin to be 'built-up'; a small pad of cotton wool is roughly moulded to the desired shape and pressed firmly against the painted area of skin, where it is 'fixed' by the adhesive power of the collodion. The cotton wool pad is then given a coat of collodion, and when dry (which should be within a few moments) is covered with foundation grease-paint.

NON-FLEXIBLE COLLODION

Non-flexible collodion, also a colourless and highly inflammable liquid, consists of pyroxylin, ether and alcohol. It is used mainly for creating artificial scars, wounds and weals. The fresh air precaution applies here too.

The main characteristic of non-flexible collodion is a remarkable power of contraction which, when the liquid is painted on any area of the skin, tends to draw the

---

* It is better not to apply collodion directly to the skin in the region of the eyes. For 'bags' under the eyes first cut two pieces of fish-skin into the desired shape, allowing about half-an-inch margin all round. Paint the area of skin to which the 'bags' are to be attached with spirit gum and when 'tacky' fix the fish-skin firmly into place. When dry, apply the collodion to the fish-skin covering and proceed to build up the 'bag.'
This procedure should also be adopted when creating 'puffy' eyelids with cotton wool and collodion. First cover the eyelid with fish-skin and create the effect over this.

flesh up into ridges and thus to form an artificial scar. It is also frequently used to draw down the corners of the mouth and eyes, etc., although I am certainly not in favour of this myself. Wherever possible, I prefer to use other means to create crows-feet or a drooping mouth; reserving non-flexible collodion solely to create the scar effects.

COLLODION AND COTTON WOOL MAKE-UP

In describing the basic highlighting and shading necessary for a youth-to-old-age make-up I have purposely refrained from mentioning the treatment for the neck area, apart from the foundation colour. The reason for this omission is twofold. In the first place a model's neck should come into a photograph only if its structural composition and the texture of the skin is more or less pleasing to the eye. I assume, therefore, that in most character studies of this type, the neck will be suitably covered. Secondly, if the neck is to be included in the photograph, then such featuring can be accomplished only by special effects, far beyond the powers of straight-forward highlighting and shading which, although satisfactory with the face, are seldom so with the neck.

The easiest and by far the cheapest of these special effects is the collodion and cotton wool make-up. Paint a small area of the skin just below the chin line with flexible collodion. Mould a small pad of cotton wool roughly into the desired shape and press it firmly against the collodion-painted area of the skin. After a few moments, when the collodion has become quite dry, apply a coat of collodion to the entire surface of the cotton wool and to a small area of the skin on each side of the pad. Mould a second pad of cotton wool and attach to one side of, and slightly overlapping the edge of, the first pad. When dry, give this second pad a coat of collodion. A third pad of cotton wool should now be

81

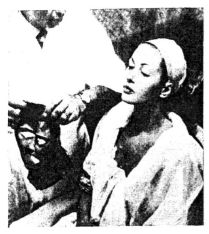

YOUTH TO AGE : 1

1 A skin-tight rubber mask, about to be placed on Yvonne De Carlo by make-up man Buddy Westmore, to give her the appearance of a 75-year old for a sequence in U-I's 'The Gal Who Took the West.'

2 Make-up man Buddy West-more and his assistant, Jack Kevan, apply the facial mask; a task requiring four hours.

3 The make-up men put the finishing touches to the facial mask.

82

4 Hair stylist, Joan St. Oegger, attends to the hair.

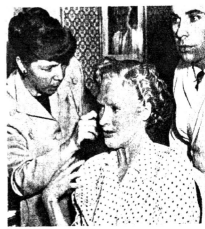

5 The make-up is carefully scrutinised before applying the finishing touches.

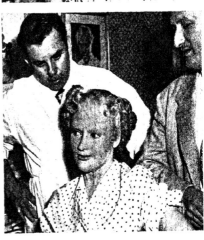

6 The completed make-up turns 25-year-old Yvonne De Carlo into a 75-year-old grandmother.

attached to the other side and slightly overlapping the edge of the centre pad, and it in turn should be coated with collodion. The pads of cotton wool must be quite small and applied with the idea of forming a double chin merging into a somewhat scrawny neck. The coating of collodion, brushed over the surface of the cotton wool, will dry within a few moments and form a thin skin covering the wool and joining on to the flesh of the neck.

The neck itself must now be 'built-up' to look thin and scrawny—a very difficult operation, and one that should be practised several times before any attempt is made to photograph the result.

Begin by painting a thin strip of collodion straight down the right-hand side of the trachea (windpipe) from a point touching, and a little to the right of, the centre pad under the chin, and finishing in the region of the clavicle or collar-bone.

Roll a four-inch strip of cotton wool between the palms of the hands until it is no thicker than a pencil, and then attach it to the painted strip of collodion, inclining very slightly outward at the upper (chin) end and slightly inwards at the lower end. The top of the cotton wool pencil must overlap the edge of the centre pad. When dry, coat with collodion. Roll a second four-inch strip of cotton wool and attach to the left-hand side of the trachea in the same way, after having painted a thin line of collodion on the surface of the skin. Incline this second strip of pencil-shaped cotton wool outwards in the opposite direction from the previous strip. As before, when dry, apply a coat of collodion to the surface of the cotton wool. Use a medium-sized flat-top sable brush for the application of collodion to the skin and a larger-sized flat-top brush for coating the cotton wool.

The two thin cotton wool pencils attached to the throat from the collar-bone to the base of the chin will, after the necessary make-up has been applied, create a realistic

AGNES MOORHEAD appears as 105-year-old Aunt Juliana in the Universal-International Picture, 'The Lost Moment,' and the following three pages show how the make-up was applied.

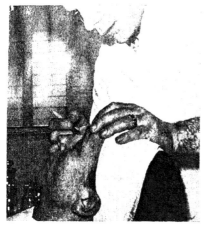

1 The lids of Miss Moorhead's eyes are painted with a diluted solution of liquid adhesive by Buddy Westmore, and are held in position whilst drying.

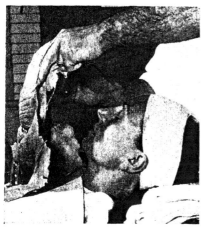

2 A skin-tight appliance is set upon the actress's face.

3 Following the placing of the face mask and prior to placing the wig, Buddy Westmore brushes Agnes Moorhead's brows with a highlight grease.

86

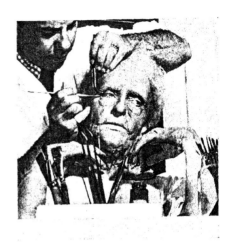

4 Make-up artist Buddy West-more puts finishing touches to the $2\frac{1}{2}$-ounce facial appliance.

5 To simulate aged and wrinkled hands. Cotton and liquid adhesive is used to build up the knuckles and fingerbones.

6 Buddy Westmore applies special rubber grease to the hands. Light and dark shades are employed to help create additional age and wrinkles.

The make-up completed, youthful Agnes Moorhead has been most effectively transformed into a 105-year-old lady. The facial appliance weighs 2½ ounces and required four hours to apply—and one hour to remove.

impression of the sternomastoids which tend to become prominent in elderly people.

If it is desired to create layers of sagging flesh around the sides of the neck, these may be fashioned from thin flat strips of cotton wool and attached with collodion in precisely the same way as the cotton wool pencils. Be sure to give each separate layer of wool a coat of collodion before applying a further layer.

Non-flexible collodion, painted or sprayed on to the sides of the neck and allowed to dry, will also create an impression of sagging flesh because the contracting action of the liquid gathers the flesh up into a series of ridges of a thickness sufficient to create the necessary illusion. Non-flexible collodion does not agree with all skins however, and to apply the liquid to such a large area of the skin is, I think, to ask for trouble. But I admit there are make-up experts who do not share my hesitation in this respect.

When all the cotton wool 'building-up' has been applied and the wool has been coated with collodion and allowed to dry, the necessary make-up must be completed. Apply the normal foundation colour to the entire neck surface including all cotton wool pads, pencils and layers. Brush-blend the colour into the crevices between the layers of the wool and also at the sides of the cotton wool pencils. Next, take a highlighting colour several shades lighter than the foundation colour, but not plain white, and run a strong highlight straight down the centre of each of the cotton wool pencils in the throat. Brush-blend these highlights with a narrow, flat-top sable brush. Add additional highlights in this way to the centres of the layers of sagging neck flesh and to the centre of the small double chin.

Now take a colour several shades deeper than the normal foundation colour and shade the sides of the throat pencils and the crevices between the layers of 'sagging flesh' cotton wool; use a small flat-top sable brush for this purpose also.

Complete the neck make-up with a normal shade of blending powder. A 'bulging' forehead (frontal bone), distorted cheek bones, and large double chins are all fashioned with cotton wool, 'fixed' with flexible collodion, and, having been coated with the same liquid, finally made-up to give the desired illusion.

CREATING SCARS AND WOUNDS

Scars are created with lip-colour and non-flexible collodion. First paint the line of the scar with lip-colour, using a spear-point sable brush if the scar is to be narrow, and a flat-top brush if a wider scar is desired. With a flat-top sable brush, paint the whole of the scar area with non-flexible collodion and allow a few moments for the liquid to dry.

Now paint a line of collodion down both sides of the red (lip-colour) line, allow it to dry, and continue to paint further layers of non-flexible collodion until the scar is the required depth. From time to time, squeeze the scar area together to assist the contracting of the flesh, and occasionally run a pointed surface, such as the reverse end of the brush, down the centre of the scar to deepen it still further.

Wounds are created in a similar way, but two different colours are used to form the basis. First paint one side of the wound area with a dark colour, then the other side with light colour. Next, apply a coat of non-flexible collodion over the surface of the wound area and, when dry, continue to build up with layers of collodion until the wound is the required depth, always making sure that each layer of liquid is quite dry before applying a further layer.

Wounds created in this way must be quite small, of course; anything in the nature of a large wound must be first fashioned with cotton wool and flexible collodion;

then made-up, and finally completed with non-flexible collodion.

Although most manufacturers of photographic cosmetics sell an Indian shade of foundation colour, I find results are far more satisfactory, from a photographic point of view, when one of the deeper shades of foundation colour is applied to the skin in the normal way and then one of the brown shading colours is blended in with the foundation to give the required tone to the skin. This method also has the great advantage of allowing the make-up artist first to select and then to create the actual tone colour which he deems most suitable for his particular lighting. The following method is widely used and permits of a good deal of control in the blending of the colours. Apply the normal foundation colour first—N.10—and blend over the surface of the face, ears and neck, down to, and including, the shoulders. Next, stipple several dabs of the special brown shading colour on to the forehead, cheeks and chin; and with the tips of the fingers smooth and blend into the foundation colour until the colour on the surface of the features is identical throughout and no trace of two different shades remains. Treat the neck and shoulders in precisely the same way, first stipple on several dabs of the shading colour and then blend in with the normal foundation until the two colours merge into one shade of a somewhat deeper tone.

A darker shade of brown should now be added to the hollows of the cheeks around the jawline and the upper eyelids. Apply the shadow to the hollow of the cheeks and blend inwards towards the nose, keeping just below the level of the cheek-bone. Extend this shadow inwards to a point about half-way between the nose and the side of the face and then blend backwards and downwards over and under the jawline. Place a few dabs of dark

91

colour on to the jawline itself and blend all the way round from ear to ear. Blend this jawline shadow upwards in a curving arc towards the upper lip from the side of the chin on both sides of the face.

The upper eyelids should be shadowed with the dark colour to create a 'deep-set' appearance. Apply the shadow fairly heavily with a flat-top sable brush and blend outwards for some distance in a straight line directly in line with the outer corners of the eyes. Also blend the shadow inwards towards the nose at the inner corners of the eyes, and upwards and over the entire surface of the upper eyelid area. Line both upper and lower eyelids with a black lining pencil and accentuate the eyebrows with a black liner.

Highlights should be applied with a flat-top sable brush practically from top to bottom of the nose. Blend this highlight slightly upwards between the eyebrows at the top and slightly downward over the tip at the base of the nose.

Highlight the line of the cheekbones at a point just below the outer corners of the eyes and carefully brush-

PAT YOUNG with Indian make-up (see page 91). Note highlighting and shading of cheeks, eyes and jawline. *Photograph by the Author*

93

blend. Highlight the frontal bone (forehead) in a curving arc pattern just above, and following the actual pattern of, the brow. Begin this highlight about half-an-inch above and exactly between the two eyebrows. The length of the highlight should be no more than an inch to an inch-and-a-half at the most. Carefully brush-blend with the foundation colour.

Highlight the chin just below the lower lip and brush-blend downwards and somewhat towards the sides. Also highlight the points of the slight dip in the flesh which run from the base of the nose to the bow of the upper lip.

Now take a pointed sable brush, charge with white colour, and with the actual point of the brush draw a fine white line on the top of the lower eyelids, touching the base of the eyelashes. Don't confuse this white line with the dark line drawn on the lower eyelids *under* the eyelashes. The white line is always drawn *above* the lashes and is a method of accentuating the whites of the eyes.

Complete the make-up by powdering *lightly*, using a suitable shade of dark blending powder for this purpose. A heavy application of powder on a character make-up of this description will completely kill the effect, so keep the powdering very much on the light side.

BALD-HEAD MAKE-UP

Bald-head effects are created by cutting a plain, white, rubber bathing cap to the side of the head and fitting it over the natural hair. The cap must be a skin-tight fit and should be 'fixed' at the front and sides with spirit gum. Liquid foundation colour is then applied to the rubber surface of the cap and the illusion completed by attaching the correct shade of crêpe hair to the sides and back with spirit gum. Pan-Cake Make-up is an excellent foundation colour for this type of effect.

For Chinese effects, always add strong additional highlights to the frontal bone, cheekbones, upper lip, and around the jawline.

Slanting eyes may be effected in the following way. Cut two one-and-a-half-inch by half-inch strips of muslin; cut one end of the muslin in the shape of a point and fold the other end over and make a small hole in the fold. Paint a small area of the flesh just beyond the outer corner of the eye with spirit gum, allow sufficient time for the gum to become 'tacky,' attach the pointed end of the muslin strip to the gummed area and fix. Attach the second muslin strip to the other eye in the same way. When dry, thread a rubber band through each of the holes in the folded end of the muslin and secure the rubber bands behind the head. Give both muslin strips a coat of flexible collodion and make up in the usual way.

		Women	Men
Pan-Cake and Pan-Stik Foundation	Blonde	N.6 or 26	N.9 or 29
	Brownette	N.5 or 25	N.8 or 28
	Brunette Dark	N.5 or N.6	N.8 or N.9
S.S. Panchromatic (Grease)	Blonde	N.6	N.9
	Brownette	N.5.	N.8
	Brunette Dark	N.5 or N.6	N.8 or N.9
Face Powder	Blonde	No. 26	No. 29
	Brownette	No. 25	No. 28
	Brunette Dark	No. 25 or 26	No. 28 or 29
Eye-shadow	Blonde	No. 21 or 22	
	Brownette	No. 6	
	Brunette Dark	No. 6	
Lip Colour	Moist Rouge No. 2 or Clear Red No. 3 For lighter tone—390A Light		Moist Rouge No. 2 mixed with 22 liner
Eyebrow Pencils	Blonde	Brown	
	Brownette	Brownish-black	
	Brunette Dark	Black	
Mascara	Blonde	Brownish-black	
	Brownette	Black or Brownish-black	
	Brunette Dark	Black	
Accessories	Removing Cream, Cotton Wool, Powder Brush, Brilliantine, Lip Brush, Highlighting Colour, Shading Colour, Astringent, Blending Brushes, (Winsor & Newton Series 52 and 53)		

LYNETTE RAE. Effective make-up calls for the correct use of cosmetics. Some suggestions are tabulated on the page opposite.

Photograph by the Author

97

SECTION FOUR

Make-up in Colour Photography

TO create a make-up suitable for a colour photograph inevitably raises fresh problems. Unfor-
tunately, the exacting nature of the whole process
of colour photography, and the fact that colour film is so
expensive, has limited experiment in this particular *genre*.
    Up to the time of writing, the majority of make-up
workers have confined their colour experiments to such
aspects as the value and intensity of colours, together
with the blending of the various coloured pigments
in an effort to achieve perfect colour harmony and
balance with the natural colouring of hair, eyes and skin
tones, etc. Although such experiments have gone a long
way towards solving the problems of colour harmony
and balance in straight and character make-up for colour
photography, the problem of corrective make-up treatment still remains to be settled; and until such time as
cosmetic manufacturers are prepared to supply precise
data upon the subject, all efforts to correct extensive
facial imperfections must remain a matter of guesswork.

CORRECTIVE MAKE-UP

This does not mean that no corrective make-up treatment is possible in colour photography. Minor adjustments may be undertaken in an effort to improve the

99

features in pretty much the same way as for a photograph taken in black and white. The difference with colour is that all such efforts are carried out on a much-reduced scale.

When applying a make-up suitable for a photograph in monochrome, the make-up artist is concerned only with the study of colour harmony and colour balance in a purely 'monochromatic' sense; his 'eye' for colour is developed and trained in such a way as to enable him, more or less, to 'sight transpose' the colour of the pigment he is using into its equivalent shade of black and white. Colours selected for contour modelling and eye-shading are chosen with a view to their ultimate reproduction as areas of varying degrees of black and white, the effectiveness of which is governed entirely by the artist's skill in application and blending. Thus errors of judgment in the application of make-up should be easy to detect and put right before the model reaches the camera. Such errors, more often than not, are all too obvious; and even if they do succeed in escaping the artist's notice they will seldom, if ever, escape the model's —who, with typical feminine 'good taste' will be quick to point out any make-up 'oddities.' For example, a too-heavy application of shading colour to the sides of the nose is not difficult to detect, especially if the shading colour is considerably darker than the foundation colour. Similarly an excess of light highlighting, insufficiently blended, will quickly draw attention to itself, if only for the reason that such extremes in contrast could not for long remain unnoticed.

In a colour photograph, however, the make-up is selected for its perfect colour harmony with the model's natural colouring rather than to correct facial imperfections. The demands of colour necessitate that, whatever make-up is used, the general effect should not be materially other than that of any well-dressed woman in her ordinary comings and goings. Extremes of contrast in the colours used are right out; and if facial correction is attempted at all, even minor correction, then it should be done with the utmost delicacy and restraint.

Any excess of highlighting or shading will completely kill the colour photograph. Models for colour photography should therefore be selected with a great deal more care than when the photograph is to be in monochrome.

APPLICATION OF MAKE-UP FOR A COLOUR PHOTOGRAPH

The latest data supplied by the Max Factor Make-up Studios in Hollywood recommends Pan-Cake Make-up for use in colour photography. It should be applied to the surface of the features with a moist sponge over an invisible make-up base after the face has been thoroughly cleansed of all street make-up, which can be easily removed by rubbing cold-cream well into the face and wiping off with face tissues or clean cotton wool. (Male models should wash with soap and water.)

After the cleansing, skin freshener should be patted lightly over the entire surface of the features with a small pad of cotton wool. This last will not only remove the greasy effect of the cold-cream but will also 'freshen up' the skin.

Max Factor Invisible Make-up Foundation is then applied in minute quantities; a small dab on the forehead, a dab on both cheeks and a final dab on the chin is quite sufficient. Blend these dabs of make-up over the entire surface of the features until no trace of the make-up remains. Now thoroughly moisten the sponge; wring some of the water from it but not all. Rub the sponge briskly around the surface of the cake until a creamy consistency is obtained. Then apply quickly, thinly and evenly to the face. Begin on the forehead, then work downwards over the surface of the face to the neck and throat until the whole of the features, from

101

the hairline to the throat, are completely covered with a thin, even film of Pan-Cake Make-up colour. With the tip of the fingers, blend the colour well up into the hairline and be particularly careful to see that it reaches the tiny smile wrinkles at the outer corners of the eyes, the inner corners of the eyes, and the crevices at the sides of the nostrils.

Sponge Pan-Cake Make-up over the features fairly quickly. This make-up is designed to provide a transparent surface, and unless it is applied quickly and thinly its whole object will be lost. A *well*-moistened sponge is the secret of success in the application of Pan-Cake Make-up.

APPLYING EYE-SHADOW

If eye-shadow is to be used apply this next. For some reason most novices appear to go slightly haywire in the application of eye-shadow. It is too often applied when it should never be applied at all; and it is even more often plastered over the eyelids with little or no thought of the consequences. It should be used only if it will materially improve the 'framing' of the eyes. In colour photography it should not be used for outdoor shots unless of the 'fashion model' type. At best, only minute quantities should be worn for full-face close-ups in colour. In no circumstances should it be used if the eyes are deep-set or 'sunken'; in such cases it only emphasises the sunken effect.

If, however, eye-shadow is deemed essential in a particular colour shot, apply it to the upper eyelids only, a fraction more heavily than the model would apply it in everyday use, but only if the picture to be taken is *not* full-face close-up. Use a flat-top sable brush; fingertip application can easily result in a far too heavy layer. Brush-blend the eye-shadow along the full length of the upper eyelids close to, and touching, the eyelashes.

102

BARBARA SUMNER with Mitzie.   *Photograph by the Author*

Leave the darkest portion of the shadow in the region of the eyelashes and blend the remainder into a fadeaway effect upwards towards the eyebrows.

The next step is to apply cheek rouge. No easy matter, this, and one which the novice would be well advised to leave entirely to the model, who will usually know precisely just where cheek rouge should be applied on her own features. Application of cheek rouge varies with each individual face; but in general the theory is that it is best applied to the high points of the cheeks and then blended along the natural curve of the cheek-bone inwards towards the nose. It should be applied with a rouge puff, or brushed on to the face with a powder brush. All edges should be blended with the finger tips into a fadeaway effect with the foundation colour. The outer portion should be blended to a point almost touching the outer corners of the lower eyelids; the inner portion blended in accordance with the structural composition of the face.

Quite a number of make-up artists do not apply powder after the features have been surfaced with Pan-Cake Make-up; and I must admit that I seldom do it myself. However, the manufacturers, Messrs. Max Factor, advise its use, so the final choice must rest with the individual worker.

Powder should be applied to the features liberally with a large, soft powder puff. It must be patted on to the surface of the skin and never rubbed or wiped on, otherwise the whole of the make-up foundation will be completely displaced. It is important that the powder reaches the inner and outer corners of the eyes and the sides of the nostrils. After applying, remove all surplus with a powder brush. First brush the surplus powder from the forehead then from around the eyes downwards over the cheeks, and over and under the chin to the throat. Even when all surplus powder has been removed, continue to brush gently until the maximum amount of smoothness has been restored to the surface of the skin.

It is a good plan to pat a little skin freshener over the surface of the skin after powdering; a few drops of the astringent on a small pad of cotton wool patted lightly over the face will prevent any grease or perspiration from forcing its way through the make-up during the actual sitting, particularly in such places as the sides of the nostrils and the corners of the mouth and eyes.

COMPLETION OF EYE MAKE-UP

Completion of eye make-up is the next step, and consists of re-shaping the eyebrows and applying mascara to the eyelashes. The eyebrows should be re-shaped with a finely pointed eyebrow pencil and every effort made to fashion the brow with a series of fine lines and never, as is sometimes attempted, to create the eyebrow with a swing or two of the pencil. Begin to work from the nose end of the brow and try tinting the actual hairs of the brow rather than the flesh in between. If the eyebrows are naturally attractive don't try to improve them; confine your efforts to following the natural curve of the brow. If it is too thin or irregular, a little cheating with the eyebrow pencil is permissible.

Wherever possible, the model should apply mascara to the eyelashes herself. Most women are sufficiently expert to do it well. But if you do decide to apply it yourself, then apply it sparingly with a brush, first brushing the lashes downwards to remove any surplus powder, then upwards over the upper eyelids. The lashes should be separated and evenly blackened with colour;

105

and black blobs of any kind should be immediately removed. The lower eyelashes should be just 'tinted' with colour; and great care must be taken to see that streaks of black do not mar the flesh underneath the eye. When this does happen, it becomes something of a problem to remove the streaks without removing all other make-up in that area as well.

RE-STYLING THE LIPS

The final stage in a make-up for a colour photograph is the re-styling of the lips. Lip-colour is applied with a lip brush. Begin work just below the bow of the lip and gradually build up the shape of the bow, working upwards. Avoid 'Cupid's bow' effects, and follow the natural line of the lip as far as possible. If too thin, the upper lip may be extended slightly; the lower lip should be full and well shaped. Do not powder the lips after lip colour has been applied.

MAKE-UP FOR MEN

It is essential that make-up should be worn by male models for all indoor colour photographs, although the make-up requirements are considerably less than for women.

No matter how closely a man may have shaved before the sitting, the skin area of beard and moustache still appears dark in comparison with the rest of his face. In black and white photography, one can always fall back upon negative retouching as a remedy for the 'blue chin' effect if the model objects to wearing a photographic make-up. Colour photography, however, does not permit of negative retouching of any description; and one is therefore dependent upon make-up.

A mild application of Pan-Stik or Pan-Cake, a spot of powder and a fairly vigorous brushing of the features with the powder brush is all the treatment necessary. If the lips are too pale they may be outlined a trifle by a very modest application of lip colour mixed with brown liner, which should be brushed on to the lips and then powdered. Men's lips, however, should never be 'shaped' or fashioned.

After applying make-up, see that eyebrows and eyelashes are free of all trace of foundation colour or powder. These can easily be removed with clean, moist cotton wool.

MAX FACTOR MAKE-UP FOR COLOUR PHOTOGRAPHY

		Women	Men
Pan-Cake	For fair skin effect	Natural 2	Tan 1
	For medium skin effect	Tan 1	Tan-Rose
	For warm skin effect	Tan-Rose	Tan-Rose
	For dark skin effect	Tan 2	Tan 2
Pan-Stik	For fair skin effect	Natural	Deep Olive
	For medium skin	Olive	Natural Tan
	For warm skin effect	Deep Olive	Natural Tan
	For dark skin effect	Golden Tan	Golden Tan
Powder	Fair	Olive	
	Medium	Olive 2	
	Dark	Tan-Rose	
Creme Rouge	Blonde	Blondeen	
	Brunette	Raspberry	
	For pink effect	Pink 1	
Dry Rouge	Blonde	Blondeen	Raspberry or Dark Technicolor
	Brunette	Raspberry	Raspberry or Dark Technicolor
	For pink effect	Pink 1	
Lipstick	Blonde	Clear Red 2	A touch of
	Brunette	See Red or	Clear Red 3
		Clear Red 3	plus 22 Liner
	For light pink effect	Pink Secret	
	For deep pink effect	Coral Glow	
Eye-Shadow	Brown or Grey, according to colour of eyes		
Eyelash Make-up	According to eyes		

SECTION FIVE

Clinical Make-up

FACIAL disfigurement, if not too prominent, need never be beyond the skill of the make-up practitioner. It can be, if not completely eliminated, at least sufficiently toned down as not to be noticeable on the subsequent print. This applies to anything ranging from 'port wine' birthmarks to the after-scars of industrial explosions. Medical men know this; and it is now common practice for a surgeon to send his patient along to the make-up studio for the final 'touches' after a drastic facial operation.

Occasionally, the portrait photographer is called upon to produce acceptable photographs of a sitter whose features are marred or disfigured in some way and who has not had the benefit of the services of an experienced make-up artist. Negative retouching is no solution. Too often in such cases the sitter's mind appears to be almost as adversely affected as his features. Photographic make-up seems, therefore, the only solution.

FACIAL DISFIGUREMENTS

Facial disfigurements fall into the following categories:

Skin pigmentations—patches of brown-coloured skin of varying size and area, with or without variation of colour.

Birthmarks—chiefly 'port wine' in colour and covering a fairly large area of the skin.

109

Effects of skin-grafting after accidents or severe burns.
Burned skin of the type which is red, hard, and shiny.
Tar and gravel marks resulting from a bad fall on the roads.
Lack of lip-line resulting from grafting of mouth.
Lack of eyebrows and eyelashes resulting from severe burning.
Sprouting eyebrows resulting from skin grafting of brow area.
Deep cuts and incisions, scars resulting from splintering glass in motor accidents, etc.
Scars from dog bites.
Scars from radium treatment.
Scars from acid burns.

MAKE-UP TREATMENT

In describing below the make-up treatment for scars, burns, and wounds, I naturally assume that these have long since healed. For obvious reasons, great care must be taken when applying make-up to the features of such sitters; powder brushes, lip-brush, eye-shadow brush and all blending brushes must be thoroughly cleansed with surgical spirit both before and after use and the same, of course, applies to the hands of the make-up artist.

A grease-paint foundation colour is usually found to be more advantageous than other types. For one thing, it is sometimes necessary—as in the case of the deeper ' port-wine' birthmark—to blend several shades of grease-paint foundation before a tone of colour is achieved which will effect an overall colour balance for the whole of the skin area. Grease-paint is the ideal medium for this type of mass blending, and I have yet to discover any other foundation cosmetic equal to the task. Another important feature is that the pigmentation of grease-paint has a 'staining' action eminently suitable for the 'fixing' of any desired coloured area or tone. Lastly, its surface is probably a little less transparent than that of other foundation cosmetics; a fact which, perhaps more than any other, should commend its use in serious clinical make-up.

TREATMENT OF BIRTHMARKS

Birthmarks of a particularly dark hue may necessitate the blending of two or more shades of foundation colour. Apply the normal foundation colour first to a small area of the dark-hued skin and closely examine the result; blend the colour from the birthmark area over on to a patch of clear skin and carefully look for any difference in tone colour. If one area appears darker than the other, blend a darker shade of colour into the light area until the two tones are perfectly matched. It is far better to blend small areas of the skin slightly darker in tone, to match the whole, rather than to increase the amount of lighter colour in an effort to 'hide' the birthmark because of the risk of creating a mask-like impression in the final print. Minor birthmarks, for the most part, completely disappear with the application of a normal foundation colour and from then on the make-up may be completed in the usual way.

TREATMENT FOR OTHER SKIN CONDITIONS

The above method of applying the foundation colour holds good for skin pigmentations, red and shiny skin, and various forms of skin-grafting, although, in the latter case, it may be necessary to use a small amount of nose putty to fill in any unevenness of the skin surface.

To remove the effect of a deep scar resulting from a bad wound, first paint the cavity with spirit gum and when 'tacky' fill the cavity with nose putty and smooth into place and level with the surrounding skin area. Paint over the nose putty with one or two coats of flexible collodion to form a new skin; keep the putty firmly in contact with the surrounding skin area; and then apply make-up in the usual way.

Sprouting eyebrows, due to grafting, should be stuck down with spirit gum in a line pointing towards the outer corners of the eyes; when dry, it will be found possible to create a more pleasing pattern of eyebrow shape with the eyebrow pencil.

The general treatment for cuts and incisions is to highlight if not too deep, and to fill with nose putty if highlighting cannot effect a cure. When nose putty is used, a coat or two of flexible collodion over the top layer of the putty will keep the putty firmly in place even if the sitter smiles.

Lack of lip-line due to grafting of mouth should be treated by first drawing the shape of the lips with a lip pencil and then 'filling in' with lip colour in the usual way.

Lack of eyelashes and eyebrows resulting from severe burning should be treated by first making-up the eyelids in the usual way then adding fine false eyelashes, which should be fixed with an adhesive.

Eyebrows should be fashioned with the eyebrow pencil in the form of a series of very fine lines drawn on the flesh itself.

Although make-up as a camouflage for facial disfigurement is practised only by a few expert photographers at the moment, the time is coming when it is likely to be the rule rather than the exception. After all, hundreds of people whose features have been marred in some way are to-day walking around in broad daylight with little or no trace of facial disfigurement because of the expert use of make-up; and there ought to be no reason why they should not feel as free to be photographed as anybody else.

I have always been glad of the chance to do jobs of this kind; not necessarily from the photographic aspect, but because a successful result always appears to give the sitter fresh confidence in himself. And that, surely, is an excellent thing in itself.

INDEX

References are for monochrome photography except where otherwise stated

113

116

ILFORD HP3

was used for all the illustrations in this book because . . .

HP3 has the right balance of colour sensitivity for modern make-up materials.

HP3 has the necessary speed for short exposures by artificial lighting.

HP3 has amazingly fine grain and gives enlargements of excellent quality.

MAKE-UP your mind to use

ILFORD *HP3*

ILFORD LIMITED · ILFORD · LONDON

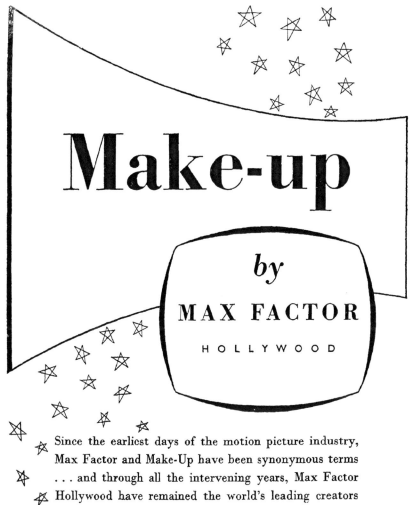

Make-up

by

MAX FACTOR

H O L L Y W O O D

Since the earliest days of the motion picture industry, Max Factor and Make-Up have been synonymous terms . . . and through all the intervening years, Max Factor Hollywood have remained the world's leading creators and advisers on every aspect of make-up for the photographic studio and for screen, stage and television.

Away from the cameras, too, Max Factor products remain the choice of the world's loveliest stars and models . . . and the make-up fashion of millions of women everywhere.

Max Factor HOLLYWOOD

The make-up for the Stars—and you

FOUNTAIN PHOTOBOOKS

PHOTOFACTS

1. The Camera	2/6	($ ·60)
2. Focusing	2/6	($ ·60)
3. Exposing	2/6	($ 60)
4. Colour Filters	2/6	($ 60)
5. Composing the Picture	2/6	($ 60)
6. Outdoor Portraiture	2/6	($ 60)
7. Landscape Photography	2/6	($ 60)
8. Seaside Photography	2/6	($ 60)
9. The Amateur's Darkroom	2/6	($ 60)
10. Developing the Film	2/6	($ 60)
11. Contact Printing	2/6	($ ·60)
12. Enlarging	2/6	($ ·60)
13. Developing the Print	2/6	($ ·60)
14. Holiday Photography	2/6	($ 60)
15. Outdoor Lighting Effects	2/6	($ 60)
16. Lantern Slides and Transparencies	2/6	($ 60)
17. Artificial Lighting	2/6	($ ·60)
18. Flash Photography	2/6	($ ·60)
19. Portraits Indoors	2/6	($ 60)
20. Action Photography	2/6	($ ·60)
21. Exposure Meters	2/6	($ 60)
22. Lenses and Shutters	2/6	($ 60)
23. Negative Faults	2/6	($ 60)
24. Print Faults	2/6	($ ·60)
25. Photographing Architecture	2/6	($ ·60)
26. Photography at Night	2/6	($ ·60)
27. Still Life Photography	2/6	($ ·60)
28. Animal Photography	2/6	($ 60)
29. Electrical Facts	2/6	($ 60)
30. Chemicals in Photography	2/6	($ 60)
31. Toning the Print	2/6	($ 60)
32. The Exhibition Print	2/6	($ 60)
Photofacts Volume I	25/-	($5·50)
Photofacts Volume II	25/-	($5·50)
Photofacts Volume III	25/-	($5·50)
Photofacts Volume IV	25/-	($5 50)

SPECIAL TECHNIQUES

Art of Photographic Salesmanship	7/6	($1·75)
Bromoil and Transfer	7/6	($1·75)
Colouring, Tinting and Toning Photographs	9/6	($2 00)
Entomological Photography in Practice	32/6	($7 95)
Exposure Meters and Practical Exposure Control	35/-	($7 75)
Focus on Architecture and Sculpture	30/-	($6 50)
Modern Enlarging Technique	12/6	($3 25)
Pearlman on Print Quality	12/6	($3·00)
Print Perfection	8/6	($2 00)
Professional Methods for Amateur Photographers	21/-	($4·75)
Synchro-flash Photography	27/6	($7·75)

COMPOSITION

Composition for Photographers	17/6	($4 00)
Pictorial Composition in Monochrome and Colour	7/6	($1 75)

CREATIVE PHOTOGRAPHY

Erith on Pictorial Photography	30/-	($6·50)
Modern Control in Photography	27/6	($6 00)
Photography and the Art of Seeing	21/-	($4·75)

COLOUR

Beginners Guide to Colour	12/6	($3·25)
Colour Before the Camera	7/6	($2·00)
Colour Separation Negatives	7/6	($2 00)
Colour Pictorial Photography	7/6	($2 00)
Colour Portraiture	7/6	($2 00)

PORTRAITURE

Baby and Camera	8/6	($2·00)
Donovan on Child Portraiture	17/6	($4·00)
Erith on Portraiture	21/-	($4·75)
Photographic Make-up	18/6	($4·25)
Successful Portraiture	6/-	($1·50)

GENERAL SUBJECTS

Box Camera Photography	1/6	($ ·40)
Boys' Book of Photography	9/6	($2·95)
Build Your Own Enlarger	8/6	($2 00)
Build Your Own Stereo Equipment	9/6	($2·95)
Camera Tips for Everyone	1/6	($ ·40)
Dictionary of Photography	21/-	($4 75)
Free-Lance Journalism with a Camera	8/6	($2·00)
Handbook of Amateur Photography	84/-	($19·50)
Hints, Tips and Gadgets for Amateur Photographers	8/6	($2·00)
How to Develop, Print and Enlarge	1/6	($ ·40)
How to Make Camera Pictures	15/-	($3·25)
How to Make a Box Camera	1/6	($ ·40)
How to Make a Vertical Enlarger	2/-	($ ·40)
How to Take Flash Pictures	1/9	($ ·40)
Photographers' Data Book	8/6	($2·00)
Photographic Exhibition Reference Book	3/6	($ ·85)
Photographer's Day in London	2/-	($ ·40)
Photographers' Guide to Better Pictures	6/-	($1 50)
Photo Digest No. 1	7/6	($2 00)
Photo Market Guide	7/6	($1·75)
Properties of Photographic Materials	35/-	($7·50)
Secret of Better Enlarging	2/6	($ ·60)
Your Camera Lens and Shutter	12/6	($3·00)

CINEMATOGRAPHY

Cine Data Book	21/-	($4·75)
Cine Hints, Tips and Gadgets	10/6	($2·75)
Cine-Film Projection	15/-	($3 75)
Handbook of Amateur Cinematography	25/-	($5·50)
Film-Strip Projection	7/6	($1·75)
Manual of Narrow-Gauge Cinematography	27/6	($6·00)
Movie Making for Everyone	9/6	($2·95)
Principles of Cinematography	63/-	($10·95)
Projectionists' Fault-finding Chart	2/6	($ ·60)
Special Effects in Cinematography	21/-	($4·75)

CINEFACTS

The Cine Camera—and How to Use it	2/6	($ 60)
Cine Film—and How to Expose it	2/6	($ ·60)
Family Movies Outdoors	2/6	($ ·60)
Travel with a Cine Camera	2/6	($ ·60)
Filming Indoors	2/6	($ ·60)
Editing and Titling	2/6	($ ·60)
The Movie Projector	2/6	($ ·60)
Home Movie Shows	2/6	($ ·60)
Making a Movie	2/6	($ ·60)
Cine Stereo for Amateurs	2/6	($ ·60)

MINIATURE PHOTOGRAPHY

Modern Portrait Technique	15/-	($3·25)
Photography with a Leica	12/6	($3·75)
35mm. Photography with an Exakta	25/-	($3 00)
35mm. Photography with a Praktiflex	15/-	($3 25)
Basic Leica Technique	19/6	($2·75)
Rollei Handbook	12/6	($2·95)
Rollei Manual	35/-	($7·50)

Send 1½d. Stamp for   *Illustrated Catalogue*

FOUNTAIN PRESS · 46/47 CHANCERY LANE · LONDON W.C.2

In U.S.A.: RAYELLE PUBLICATIONS
5700 Oxford Street, Philadelphia 31, Pa.

Printed in the United Kingdom by
Lightning Source UK Ltd., Milton Keynes
141778UK00001B/69/A

9 781406 744842